The Novels of Bhabani Bhattacharya

The Novels of Bhabani Bhattacharya

BALRAM S. SOROT

PRESTIGE

Published by
Prestige Books
3/28, East Patel Nagar, New Delhi 110 008
in association with
Indian Society for Commonwealth Studies
New Delhi

ISBN: 81-85218-31-5

Phototypesetting by
Laser Impressions
New Delhi 110 028
Ph. 537296, 537756

Jacket design by
Three-A Corporation
New Delhi 110 002

Printed at
Mehra Offset Press
New Delhi 110 002

Contents

Preface

The Indian Novel in English, about a hundred years old now, can boast of maturity, with a number of talented Indian writers trying their hand at fiction in English. Novelists like K.A. Abbas, Mulk Raj Anand, R.K. Narayan, Raja Rao, Kamala Markandaya, Anita Desai, Manohar Malgonkar, Nayantara Sahgal, Salman Rushdie and Ruth Jhabvala have been widely acclaimed as high ranking creative artists. Ironically enough, these men of letters were recognized in their own homeland long after they won reputation abroad.

Bhabani Bhattacharya, one of the leading Indian English novelists of older generation, though widely popular abroad, has also suffered a comparative neglect in his own country. While Twayne Publishers, Boston, included him for critical evaluation in "World Authors Series," Indian scholars have failed to bring out any serious critical study of his works. The monographs of K.R. Chandrasekharan and K.K. Sharma, entitled *Bhabani Bhattacharya* and *Bhabani Bhattarcharya: His Vision and Themes* respectively, though creditable as introductory studies, hardly succeed to provide an in-depth critical assessment of Bhabani Bhattacharya's genius and art. There are various aspects of the novelist which still require intensive evaluation from different points of view.

The present study attempts to fill up a serious gap in the Bhattacharya criticism by highlighting one of the most important aspects of his novels and short stories: the blending of the traditional and the modern values. This critical approach is particularly significant for it helps to give a deeper insight into the creative process of Bhabani Bhattacharya.

The last chapter is devoted to an analysis of the general characteristics of Bhattacharya as a novelist. Though not directly connected with the leitmotif of the present study, it has been included because of its relevance to the overall assessment of the author's art and technique.

Introduction

Bhabani Bhattacharya (1906-89) was born on November 10, 1906, at Bhagalpur, Bihar. He had his early education at various places where his father, Promotho Bhattacharya, served, and later went to Patna for his college education. He graduated with honours in English Literature from Patna University in 1927, and thereafter left for London for higher studies. Though interested in pursuing his studies in English literature at King's College, University of London, he was advised to study History. He, therefore, first completed the Bachelor's degree with honours in History and then took Ph.D degree in the same subject from the University of London in 1934.

Bhabani Bhattacharya was a precocious child and started writing at a very early age. He was only twelve when one of his early efforts appeared in the famous children's magazine, *Mouchak*. At the age of nineteen, he won a competition that was held to select poems for inclusion in Tagore's *Chayanika*. He pursued his creative activities during his studies in London too, and in 1932, published *The Golden Boat*, a small book containing English translations by him of some of Tagore's poems and anecdotes.

After completing his studies in England, Bhattacharya returned to India. In the following year (1935), he was married to Salila Mukherjee. A good short-story writer in her own right, Salila helped Bhattacharya a great deal in his literary pursuits. In 1944, he published *Indian Cavalcade* – a collection of various articles – presenting a panorama of Indian history to the readers. This book may be treated as the earliest of Bhattacharya's attempts in creative writing. The short pieces of *Indian Cavalcade*, though dealing with historical personages, are much like imaginative short-stories. From then onwards, Bhattacharya delved deeper and deeper into the realm of creative writing, and the year 1947 saw him publish his first novel, *So Many Hungers,* which established his reputation as a promising Indian English novelist.

He worked as a Press Attache at the Embassy of India in Washington, D.C. in 1949, and a year after became the Assistant Editor of *The Illustrated Weekly of India*. Encouraged by the overwhelming success of his first novel, Bhattacharya started writing vigorously. Taking up the theme of the clash between tradition and modernity in Indian social life, he brought out his second novel, *Music for Mohini,* in 1952. With the publication of his third novel, *He Who Rides a Tiger,* in 1954, his reputation as a leading Indian English novelist was firmly established. He travelled extensively in the years to come, and was closely associated with the literary activities outside India. He represented India at the Harvard International Seminar at Cambridge, Massachussetts, in 1959, and in the following year, went to Tokyo to participate in another International Seminar on literature. By the time his fourth novel, *A Goddess Named Gold,* was published (1960), Bhattacharya had been recognized both in India and abroad as a reputed literary artist. The Government of India appointed him Consultant to the Ministry of Education in 1961. The same year he contributed to the preparation and publication of the Tagore centenary volume, *Towards Universal Man*, in the capacity of Editor-cum-Chief Translator of the book.

During the two succeeding years he toured New Zealand, Australia and West Germany extensively and lectured there in various universities. In 1962, he received the "Universities of New Zealand's Prestige Award" for his writings. His famous novel, *Shadow from Ladakh,* was published in 1966. It was widely acclaimed and was awarded Sahitya Akademi Prize in 1967 for being the year's best creative work in English. Besides novels, Bhattacharya also wrote short stories which were published in 1968 under the title: *Steel Hawk and Other Stories.*

In 1969, Bhattacharya published *Gandhi the Writer: the Image as it Grew* to mark the birth centenary of Gandhi. In this book, he threw light upon Mahatma Gandhi as a writer. The same year he joined East-West Centre, Honolulu, as a senior specialist, and the following year he was appointed Visiting Professor at the University of Hawaii. In 1973, Bhattacharya became Walker-Ames Professor at the University of Washington, Seattle, and also started working on a new novel.

In 1977, Bhattacharya brought out another book, *Mahatma Gandhi*, which though largely based upon his earlier work, *Gandhi the Writer,* also dealt with Gandhi's political, philosophical and socio-economic ideas. His last novel, *A Dream in Hawaii,* which portrays the East-West cultural encounter, was published in 1978. Notwithstanding his advanced years, he brought out *Socio-Political Currents in Bengal: A 19th*

Century Perspective, a non-fiction work in 1980. Bhattacharya thus continued to write till his death, in October 1989.

Rabindranath Tagore and John Steinbeck are the most prominent among the writers who left their deep imprint on the mind and art of Bhabani Bhattacharya. Acknowledging his debt to them, he writes:

> Tagore appealed to me from my school days and my writer's career also began from those days. It was therefore quite unlikely that I would miss the impact of Gurudev's all pervading personality. Later I read many English and American authors. Among those John Steinbeck attracted me most.[1]

Bhattacharya not only studied the works of Tagore with devotion, but also translated in English some of his short-stories and sketches collected in *The Golden Boat* and *Towards Universal Man*. The peculiarities of Tagore's style and technique – lucidity, suggestiveness and economy of words – have become integral to Bhattacharya's own way of writing, and the impact of these attributes may clearly be traced in his short-stories. Some of Tagore's philosophical ideas, such as the idea of the integration of diverse elements in human life and his aesthetic views, have also been elaborately treated in Bhattacharya's *Music for Mohini* and *Shadow from Ladakh.*

John Steinbeck, too, left a great impress on the art and ideas of Bhattacharya. Steinbeck's concern for social justice, his interest in common man, his fusion of moral earnestness with sardonic humour, his style of mixing fact with fantasy, his mild irony tinged with humour, and his comic detachment are some of the significant characteristics from which Bhattacharya drew a great deal of inspiration. The impact of Steinbeck in matters of themes and their treatment is perceptible in Bhattacharya's novels like *So Many Hungers* and *He Who Rides a Tiger*. In both of these novels, the writer vividly portrays the social injustice and raises a strong voice in protest against it. He, however, views society and man-in-society from a distance, and writes objectively, though sympathetically. In his style, too, Bhattacharya fairly draws from Steinbeck's method of using irony tinged with mild satire. The delicate and subtle irony plays over the structure treated in most of his stories as is evidenced by "Glory at Twilight," "My Brave Great-Uncle," "Names Are Not Labels," and "A Moment of Eternity."

Besides Tagore and Steinbeck, Mahatama Gandhi also left his impact on Bhattacharya's mind and ideas. The Gandhian view of life figures prominently in each of his first five novels. *So Many Hungers* deals with Gandhi's influence on the Freedom Struggle. It upholds the Gandhian ideas of non-violence and passive resistance. *Music for Mohini* pleads for rural uplift, social re-construction and adult education as preached and practised by Gandhi in his life. *He Who Rides a Tiger* fosters the cause of the poor and the down-trodden for whom Gandhi fought undauntedly and untiringly. *A Goddess Named Gold* envisages Gandhian vision of economic development in free India. In *Shadow from Ladakh*, Bhattacharya pleads for the synthesis of Gandhian values of moral regeneration and modernism born in the wake of scientific and technological development. Regarding Gandhi's impact on Bhattacharya's fiction, Dorothy Blair Shimer observes: "Those acquainted with Bhattacharya's own creative writing must acknowledge the influence Gandhi has had on his work. All the Bhattacharya novels are rooted in Gandhian philosophy, and all deal predominantly with 'the common man' in a 'simple, direct, and natural' manner."

Gandhi's profound influence on Bhattacharya is also evidenced by the fact that he has written two books on Gandhi, *Gandhiji the Writer* (1969) and *Mahatma Gandhi* (1977), in which he not only shows how Gandhi paved the way for the writers of his age, but also discusses some of his political and philosophical views. Describing Gandhi's powerful influence on Indian writers, Bhattacharya remarks:

> Inspired by him, they turned towards the depiction of the life of the common man, the poor and the illiterate, particularly in the villages. Their prose style became less ornamental, less designed for the highbrow scholar.... There was a reaction against obsolete values. The writers drew largely on life for their themes and new horizons opened up before them.[3]

Since Bhattacharya was actively contemplating a creative writer's career for himself in the forties, he too was obviously influenced by Gandhi's writings. The two important attributes of Gandhi's style—directness and simplicity—are manifestly discernible in Bhattacharya's style also.

Bhattacharya had started his literary activities while studying in England. It was the time when diverse forces reacted upon his young mind. Lila Ray refers to these when she remarks: "He joined the Junior P.E.N. Club in London and associated himself with the progressive movements of the time. He was an Anti-Fascist."[4] The contact with the progressive writers of England brought him in touch with the Marxist ideology and made him aware of the basic causes behind the pitiable lot of the downtrodden. The sympathy for the proletariat, the plea for an equal distribution of wealth in society, and the vehement appeal for the elimination of caste and class discrimination – all these essential attributes of the progressive view of life – have convincingly been put forward by him in his novels, *So Many Hungers*, *He Who Rides a Tiger* and *A Goddess Named Gold*. It was because of the manifestation of the progressive views in his writings that when he visited Russia, "the audience rose to its feet as he appeared, acclaiming him with thunderous applause."[5]

The prevailing social conditions also worked upon the growing mind of Bhattacharya, and inspired him to create his first novel. The famine of 1943 which stalked through the sacred soil of Bengal, was one of such events as he himself confesses:

> Then the great famine swept down upon Bengal. The emotional stirrings I felt (more than two million men, women and children died of slow starvation amid a man-made scarcity) were a sheer compulsion to creativity. The result was the novel *So Many Hungers*.[6]

Bhattacharya could also not escape the impact of the social environment in which he was brought up and grew to maturity. The spirit of the age – the world-wide demands for equality, liberty and fraternity, and the growing unrest among Indian masses to liberate themselves from the alien rule, fired his imagination and impelled him to write.

The historical events in India which formed the background of Bhattacharya's writings and influenced them powerfully can be divided in two phases: the first phase stretches from World War II to Independence and the second from Independence to the late seventies. The social, political and economic conditions of both these historical phases are reflected in his writings.

When the Second World War broke out, the popular Ministries which had been voted to power by sweeping majority in the election of 1937 resigned as a protest against the British Government's dragging India in the War without consulting the Indian legislature. When the Congress failed to resolve the constitutional deadlock through parleys and conferences with the Viceroy, it embarked upon the Individual Civil Disobedience Movement in 1940. The Congress did not think it desirable to embarrass the British Government engaged in its life and death struggle against Fascist powers by starting mass Civil Disobedience movement. Finding the alien Government unrelenting, and sensing the danger from the advancing forces of the Japanese in South-East Asia, the Congress passed on August 8, 1942, the famous "Quit India" resolution demanding the withdrawal of the British Powers from India and sanctioning a mass struggle on non-violent lines on the widest possible scale under the leadership of Gandhi. The Congress was, however, soon banned and all its great leaders including Gandhi were put behind bars. In the absence of any popular leadership, the masses of India, who rose in rebellion owing to the arrest of their leaders, resorted to violent riots and assaults, sporadic disorders, and acts of sabotage on a large scale in different parts of India. For days, the administration in certain areas seemed paralyzed. The imperialist Government adopted strong measures of repression including firing from aeroplanes. These callous repressive measures were followed by drastic penalties and punitive fines on individuals and groups.

Gandhi voiced from jail his emphatic protest against the heinous cruelties and heavy penalties on Indian masses, and finding the Government indifferent to miseries of the people undertook a twenty-one day fast at the age of seventy-four. The whole country was plunged in a nerve-racking anxiety, and as his life hung by a thread, there was a country-wide agitation for his release. Meanwhile, the War ended in 1945 and the Labour Party, which came into power in Britain, made sincere efforts to end the political deadlock in India. On the basis of the political settlement reached in 1947 between the British Government and the Indian leaders, India was partitioned and the dominions of India and Pakistan were established on August 15, 1947.

India witnessed profound and far-reaching changes in its economic life during this period. The growing demand for war materials both at home and other parts of the Commonwealth, and assistance on the part of the Government with regard to industries, contributed to increased activity and output in all items of industrial manufacture. However, the conditions of peasants and common people, which had shown signs of great improvement as a result of progressive measures introduced during the Congress Ministries, suffered a great setback after the Ministries resigned, and the rigours of the war-time increased. There was a rapid rise in the prices of all goods and a drastic reduction in the supply of essential commodities, particularly food grains and cloth, to the civilian population. Notwithstanding all measures of control, regulation of price, Government procurement and distribution of essential supplies and rationing system prices continued to soar, black markets flourished and corruption increased. The most harrowing tragedy India witnessed because of the scarcity of food and war conditions was the unprecedented famine in Bengal. Millions died of starvation – a greater number than the total British empire casualties in the War. In the large areas of Bengal, family life was uprooted, whole classes of artisans and agricultural labourers were wiped out, and social and moral disintegration set in. The wounds inflicted on Bengal by this terrible calamity were very slow to heal.

India faced many problems of serious magnitude in the wake of its emergence as an independent country. The freedom was born in the hour of communal disturbances of unprecedented ferocity and unbelievable bestiality. Millions of people had to flee leaving their homes and property, nearly half a million were killed, and over a lac women, young and old, were abducted, raped and mutilated. It was the shame and agony of the partition, the glory as well as the defeat of the hour of freedom. Added to this was the shocking assassination of Mahatma Gandhi and the unprovoked attack on Kashmir by Pakistan. The attack by Pakistan came when the Indian Government was busy in solving the Herculean problems of the rehabilitation of millions of refugees and the integration of the scattered and unfriendly princely states in the Indian Union. Indian leaders faced these problems with sagacity and courage, and went ahead with their plans to establish political and economic stability in the country, and usher in a new era of hopes and aspirations. On January 26, 1950, India became a republic and opted for secular democracy with socialism as its goal. Since then it had been making all out efforts to speed up the industrialization in the country to lead it to its onward march on the road of progress. Though the aggressions on its borders by Pakistan and China have attempted to destabilize and damage its political and economic set-up, India has remained undaunted in its efforts to advance itself to the front rank of the developed countries.

After the ushering in of the Independence, India had to take some significant decisions about the reorganization of its social and economic structures. With regard to its social set-up, it had to make a choice between the two extremes of the blind adherence to old Indian traditions and the unthinking imitation of the Western materialistic civilization. It has wisely decided to bring about a synthesis of the best in the two cultures. While keeping itself rooted in its old ethical traditions, it is trying to develop modern scientific outlook on life and reorganize its social set-up by ridding it of its superstitions, casteism, and communalism. In the economic sphere it has opted for industrial and technological progress as opposed to relying merely on indigenous cottage industries and decentralized economy.

Bhabani Bhattacharya, who has witnessed these significant turning-points in the life of his country with keenness, has tried to delineate them in his novels and short stories artistically. Reconciling his art with the native social and cultural commitments, Bhattacharya weaves the web of his fiction round the contemporary historical events and social conditions. As he is alive to the social, economic and political changes that India has been undergoing from time to time, he is also interested in analyzing the historical forces working behind these changes.

Bhattacharya depicts life in Indian society exactly as he has viewed it with a discerning eye. His themes are close to social reality and based on real experience. He is concerned with large public issues and social problems. He generally writes about the poverty, hunger, pestilence, traditionalism and the resulting controversy of Gandhian panacea versus rapid industrialization. In this way, he touches almost all the aspects of the present-day India while weaving a pattern for the stories of his novels.

The first five novels of Bhabani Bhattacharya, *So Many Hungers* (1947), *Music for Mohini* (1952), *He Who Rides a Tiger* (1954), *A Goddess Named Gold* (1960), and *Shadow from Ladakh* (1966) which won Sahitya Akademi award, are set against the background of the changes in the political, economic and social life in India. *So Many Hungers* depicts the Bengal Famine of 1943. *Music for Mohini* attempts a synthesis of eastern and western cultures. *He Who Rides a Tiger* not only champions the cause of the poor and down-trodden but also records the cruelty of the rich at the time of war. *A Goddess Named Gold* presents the problems that India faced about the dawn of independence. *Shadow from Ladakh* takes a more kaleidoscopic view of Indian society right from the independence to the Chinese aggression. In these novels, Bhattacharya describes the horrors of war and famine, pestilence, clash of traditions, ignorance, misguided faith in religion, superstitions, casteism, and economic and food crisis. The sixth and the last of Bhattacharya's novels, *A Dream in Hawaii* (1978), deals with the East-West encounters by juxtaposing Indian spiritualism with Western materialism and uses both India and the island of Hawaii for its setting.

So Many Hungers is one of the finest pieces of creative writing born out of the agonized torment of body and spirit endured by the sacred soil of Bengal during the hideous famine years and the early stages of the Second World War. It portrays vividly the Quit India movement of 1942, the mass uprisings, acts of sabotage which followed in its wake, the indiscreet and the distressing scenes of human misery and degradation resulting from famine which stalked through the land and killed millions of people. While describing the wrath of Indian masses who, roused to bitter indignation at the arrest of national leaders, indulged in acts of violence and paralyzed the government machinery in towns and villages, Bhattacharya writes:

> For ten days the city was in the grip of revolt. A sudden thunderstorm on a dark, deadly gulf of Time? For at that moment the Jap stood firm on the doorstep of Bengal, poised for attack. The national movement could no longer wait and watch the peril and mark time.[7]

The British who boast of their faith in the "four freedoms" and "the rights of man," unleash the reign of terror in India and resort to inhuman atrocities on Indians to repress their struggle for freedom. "Authority was bent on smashing every vestige of the movement which it had now outlawed. Authority was goading, provoking the movement so that patience lost, it would expose itself, target for gunfire." (67) While in theory the British talk of their "respect for the rights of all people to choose the form of government under which they shall live," in practice they shamelessly crush the just aspirations of Indians to breathe in free India. Actually, "the champions of freedom abroad were the eaters of freedom in this land." (40) They think that they had conquered their Indian Empire by the sword, and by the sword they will hold it.

The novel also portrays the hardships faced by the common man during the war. The fishing boats of villagers are seized by the Government for the use of military personnel and villagers are led to sell grain to the agents of the imperialist government, greedy merchants and hoarders. To the businessmen like Samarendra Basu and Sir Ablabandhu, war comes like a veritable windfall. They treat it as the chance of a life-time. As the war progresses, they accumulate rice in their granaries and hoard it to sell at a higher price later. While describing the din and clamour in the Calcutta Stock Exchange, the author writes:

> Chance slipping off. Chance of twenty years. Not another war for twenty years. War, the most enriching industry. Prices mounting. Steels the favourite counter. The crowd surging. Bee voices buzzing for money-honey. (17)

Greedy and callous men, and freakish nature join hands to cause famine in Bengal. Bhattacharya gives a very detailed, graphic and moving picture of the hunger for food and the heavy loss of human lives resulting from it. Famine shows such distressing pictures of human sufferings as men have never witnessed before. Mothers unable to bear the death by starvation of their children, bury them alive. Women sit on the pavement eating from a bowl while their famished children sit by and gaze. Men keenly waiting for their turn to get food, breathe their last the moment food is poured in their bowl. There are sights such as make man's blood curdle with horror:

> The jackal had eaten the woman's left armpit and breast, and a part of the ribs. She was breathing still, her eyes wide open but vacant. (146)

We are shown how hunger and starvation reduce people to the levels of animals:

> Destitutes and dogs in those days often fought for possession of the rich city's ten-thousand rubbish-heaps, in which craps of

> rotting food lay buried. It was not every time that the destitutes won, routing the dogs on the streets and the dog within themselves. (178)

Juxtaposed with this woeful tale of man's hunger for food is the hateful sight of man's callous greed for wealth. While the granaries of the selfish and greedy capitalist and black-marketeers like Sir Ablabandhu and Samarendra Basu abound in rice, innumerable human beings die for want of it. While the restaurants of the rich city, Calcutta, buzz with life and music, and bulge with food, destitutes in the nearby lanes and on the pavements lie sick and helpless and die of hunger. In this world of wealthy traders, there prevails a callous disregard of all codes of civilized humanity.

If the famine exposes the sordidness and meanness of human soul, it also brings on surface its hidden springs of nobleness. As opposed to the callous and greedy rich people, the helpless and famished destitutes rise above their bodily needs and reveal a hidden core of sympathy and heroism. A semi-starved destitute surrenders his ticket for food so that a more needy man may use it. A peasant girl abuses the body's sanctity to feed starving destitutes who call her "mother." A famished boy, who has fought against a dog to procure a jam tin lying in a dust-bin, shares his treasure with a youngster looking with pitiful eyes towards him. Bhabani Bhattacharya has thus immoratlized in this novel the memory of the hideous famine years in all its sordidness, in all its shadow and shimmer.

In *Music for Mohini,* Bhattacharya takes us close to the year of Indian independence and discusses the problem of country's social regeneration. The theme of the novel is struck by the solitary musings of its hero, Jayadev:

> India was on the verge of freedom: a new page of world history was writing itself. The political implications were visible to all but not the social problems. What was political liberty worth to the common man if it was not part of a renanscence in social life.[8]

Having lived in a village, Jayadev knows that the Indian society, particularly in the villages, is caught in the deadly mire of obscurantism, superstitions, ritual and obsolete customs, and defies all attempts at its reformation. Describing the pitiable condition of the putrid Indian society, he reflects:

> Society, rural society (and nine-tenths of India was rural) was sick with taboos and inhibitions of its own making: the iniquities of the caste and untouchability; the ritualism that passed for religion; the wide-flung cobweb of centuries of decadence. The purity of ancient thoughts had been lost in misinterpretation until the dignity of man had become a mere plaything of vested interest. (67-68)

The village, Behula, and its Big House to which Jayadev belongs, represent India with its social putrefaction caused by the centuries of blind faith and iron traditions. Just as the social reform of India is made difficult by the stubbornness of its obscurantist people, so does the Big House of Behula defy any changes in its traditional set-up because of the eccentricities of Jayadev's iron-willed mother. She is suspicious of her son's attempts at modernizing the village, Behula, and introducing social reforms in it. Her superstitious faith gets a jolt when she learns that her daughter-in-law, Mohini, whom she has suspected of being barren, is able to bear the child even without appeasing the Virgin Goddess. She relents in her attitude and also gets reconciled to the changes introduced in the village by Jayadev and his modernized doctor friend, Harindra.

The story of *He Who Rides a Tiger* is also cast in the background of the Bengal famine and the Quit India movement. We learn of hungry destitutes going to the city in the futile search for work and food, and famished men and women dying of hunger. Innocent girls are lured to the city to turn harlots to save themselves from starvation. Corpses of destitutes are stripped off skin and flesh, and skeletons are shipped to far off countries across the black-waters to satisfy the needs of medical students there. Processions of political volunteers demanding food for the hungry are chased and beaten mercilessly by cruel-hearted policemen. We hear the chorus of lamentation of men and women wailing together, "Save us from the slaughter," as they are being forcibly taken out of the big city in military trucks. Giving an account of the beginning of famine in Bengal during war years, Bhattacharya writes:

> The dark year started three or four months after Chandra Lekha won her silver medal. It was almost the darkest in the history of Bengal. A plague took the land in its grip, the plague of hunger, in the wake of war.
>
> 1943 !
>
> The Japanese army stood poised at the eastern front, facing a wall of resistance. But no barricades had been put up against the enemy within the borders: no checking of the giant sharks who played the cornering game on a stupendous scale. Barns were empty—the peasants had been induced to sell off their grain. Markets were empty—the grain was hidden away. The tillers of the soil, reduced to starvation, had no recourse but to sell land. And now rice was five times the old rate.
>
> Weavers sold their looms to traders for big cities who scoured the countryside for bargains. Artisans sold their tools. Fishermen's boats were chopped up for firewood to sell. The plague washed up in fierce tides. Bengal was dying.[9]

How the starvation makes the people selfish and hard-hearted, is conveyed by Kalo who sees:

> one destitute man thrust his fingers into the mouth of another, force it open, scoop out bread and lump the masticated mass into his own mouth, while the victim beat helplessly with his thin sticks of arms and blubbered. (124-25)

The novel also depicts the rebellious temper of the people of India who, enraged by famine and inhuman atrocities on freedom-fighters, take out processions and demonstrate against the alien government:

> Food! Food! Food for the hungry! The cry filled the air of the great city. Something had seized the people so that their apathy was broken. Great demonstrations were to be seen in the streets almost everyday. (167)

Describing the political awakening among Indian masses, Biten remarks:

> There are deep stirrings in the country. People who have slept for centuries are sitting up, feeling the chains on their legs. When they

> are fully awake and the strength surges in their limbs, they will snap the chains with a mighty effort. (170)

The novel also exposes the wicked practices of the hollow religion, employed by the vested interests to exploit the blind faith of simple and credulous people. Religion seems to have lost its pristine glory and forgotten its basic ethical values. It is turned into a spiritual trade where people try to buy spiritual merit in exchange for merchandise:

> Food for the soul is produced and sold like food for the stomach, and though the ways of the two trades are different, you pay for both with hard cash. The temple is a market and the priest a dealer. People are always ready to pay well for feeding the inner man! (43)

The cheats and the sharks – the pot-bellied jute merchants and rice-profiteers like Sir Ablabandhu and rich stock-brokers like Motichand – become the upholders of religion and use it for their selfish gains. The novel satirizes the blind religious faith of ignorant masses who grudge to feed famished destitutes, but fill wholeheartedly the alms-bowls of the *sadhus*. Equally bitter is the author's indictment of the misguided devotees who turn a deaf ear to the cries of children dying of hunger, but donate buckets of milk for the bath of the idol of the temple.

In *A Goddess Named Gold*, Bhabani Bhattacharya draws a vivid picture of India just before the advent of freedom. People's patriotism, enthusiasm and expectations, notwithstanding immediate fears and doubts about the results of the newly-won independence, find artistic expression in this novel. With freedom in sight – barely a hundred days left to end two hundred years's alien rule and enact the historic events of India's freedom – people are found to be full of excitement and thrill: "Ho ! A hundred days left until we are free – free! 'Think of it and the breath stops in each nostril, then blows fast – faster.'"[10] Even the illiterate womenfolk in the villages are full of joyous spirit. They are confident that the "British Lion," who with tail between his legs is about to leap across the oceans to his homeland, cannot delay their freedom which is only a hundred days ahead. People are full of enthusiasm about the economic re-construction of free India. Sohan Lal inquires of Meera and her Grandma if they have ever used the factory-made "white manure." When they utter a confused "No" for their answer, he declares with a light in his eyes:

> Wait till freedom comes and bagfuls of the new manure will be rushed to every field. Then the very face of India will change. The people are going to be the masters. It is they who will own everything. The land, the rivers, the railways. (114)

While focussing on the hopes and aspirations of the Indian masses at the time of national independence, the author also expresses their doubts and fears. The common masses are fully aware of the dangers likely to be let loose by the exploiters, the money-lender and the glib-tongued politicians who may try to misuse the newly-won freedom for their own selfish and mean ends. Musing over the danger apprehended by the country from the greedy traders and unscrupulous politicians, Sohan Lal observes:

> Yes, there were the robbers, Seths of many kinds. The cities had a greater variety and profusion of them than the countryside. There was the money-Seth, of course, to whom freedom meant a chance to seize fields of trade vacated by the aliens. Then the Seth of politics, ready to dupe the people with the power of his glib tongue. The official Seth, a man of arrogance ready to change masters without a change of mentality, human chattel open to the best offer. The Seth of religion with Gods for sale. The Seth with a Gandhi cap on his head and the cap itself a deceit. And several others on the list. (119)

The advent of freedom makes people conscious of their rights. Meera, the heroine of the novel, echoes this resurgent spirit when she remarks: "Equal rights from men and women, that was the song. We had to fight for that song" (148) Describing the feelings of the common masses who have a deep faith in free India, the author points out: "The days of the Seths were numbered. Soon would the people, vested with their new power, fully waken and their thunderous wrath would make every tyrant whine for mercy." (224)

Shadow from Ladakh, written with the backdrop of Indo-China flare-up of 1962, records the pulse-beats of Indian society which deviates from the Gandhian ideology. It presents a survey of the pre- and post-Independence era in the history of India. The difference between the two periods is brought out through the conflict between Satyajit and Bhashkar, not merely a clash of personalities, rather a historical inevitability that was bound to come to the fore sooner or later. The Chinese aggressions put the conflicts in focus, hastening the process of self-discovery. India might have gone on sleeping for decades together, had Mao Tse-Tung not betrayed her in 1962. Suddenly, India was faced with the problems of choice between idealism and practical wisdom, the outdated and the modern.

The novel deals with the fundamental issues involved in the regeneration of the country, i.e. the choice of ideals on which free India is to be nourished. Has it to follow the path of non-violence, asceticism and village economy or to take the West-influenced modern ways of power, machine and industrialism? Gandhi or Nehru – in whose image India is to be shaped? Bhattacharya records this ideological tussle of the contemporary India in the novel. The discussion between Satyajit and Bhashkar that takes place in the opening pages of the book, reveals the spirit of the times: the conflict between Gandhian ideology and modern outlook, and the dire need of the times – to change, to break away from the old ways of life. Bhashkar reacts sharply to Satyajit's ironic and sentimental indictment of large-scale steel production, and remarks:

> There is no room today for that kind of sentimentality. It's question of our survival. We have to get steel, more and more, at any price. The pace of production must quicken.[11]

He further adds:

> You have given yourself to your ideals. But that is beside the point, sir. Here is a simple question from accelerated production. Know-how. Latest techniques. Planning. Blueprints. You have to stand aside and let us do our job. (31)

Besides this ideological conflict, India had to face the Chinese attack in 1962. The novel brings to light the great shock that India receives by this attack of a friendly neighbouring country:

> The country had been struck first with horror, then grief, and when, after negotiations, a helicopter landed at New Delhi with the remains of nine uniformed bodies preserved in Himalayan ice,

> there was an explosion of great fury. The funeral pyre consuming dead flesh also burned off the *bhai-bhai* slogan that had lived in millions of hearts in city and country, factory and farm, mansion and hovel. A little ash alone remained of the page on which a great friendship had been inscribed. (66)

Slowly and menacingly, the Chinese army had been advancing amid the snow-covered mountains for several past years. They had constructed Aksai-Chin Road just to trespass a vast area of Indian territory without paying any heed to the genuine protest of the Indian Government. Bhattacharya makes a documentary report of these historic events:

> That was the shape of the events of the winter of 1959. History in the subsequent year had moved fast. The old mask of friendship on the Chinese face had been replaced by one that scowled. If India valued the goodwill of her neighbour, she must accept all Chinese claims. (167)

The author also gives a vivid and graphic description of the massive attack by the Chinese army:

> The Chinese had overwhelming superiority in numbers and firepower. Their infantry was armed with automatic weapons. Attacking in successive waves supported by heavy mortars, they used the human-sea technique, as in Korea. Indian troops defended every inch of ground, but, as a foreign correspondent said, they had little to fight except with great courage. (242)

In his last novel, *A Dream in Hawaii*, Bhattacharya exposes the hollowness of the materialistic American society suffering from the deep-rooted value-crisis. The following words of Stella Gregson throw light on the moral degradation of the American society:

> Our American society with its contradictions! Violence in its most brutal forms rages through the nation and tries to destroy every civilized norm. Yet a great search goes on widening, the search for . . . shall I say, a new world aching to be born?[12]

In this society, dominated by money, sex and violence, the old and established moral values hardly find any place. Talking about the values which prevail in the modern American society, Frieda tells Yogananda:

> Men need to be liberated the same way as the women. We must all be equally free to achieve all sexual self-discovery. That's what the current moral revolution amounts to, briefly stated. (108-9)

She further points out:

> All America is experiencing a sex completion. The old lifeways are gone; they've left a sort of emotional mess, but out of that mess new attitudes arise – fast.(109)

The Swami feels stunned as she elaborates American modernity:

> She was intent on broadening his knowledge of American society. The death of worn-out sanctities. Marriage reduced to a convenient contract. For the young and unmarried, dating and mating were the same. Virginity became a sin when you were over sixteen. Virgin girls and virgin boys beyond their teens were all too rare anyhow. (109)

Commenting on the morbidness, immorality and inhumanity of the modern society of the super-technological America, Yogananda remarks:

> Western society is imperilled by its self-induced venom called progress. Implied in that progress is science destroying as much as it creates! Implied equally is the loss of humanness. It's hard to evade the question: Is this the death march of Western life? The spiritual nature in Western man – is it lost for all time? (117-18)

Through his talks and dialogues, the Swamy impresses upon the youths of America the value of the gospel of the *Bhagavat Gita*, of desireless action to attain inner adjustment and peace. He exhorts them to strive for God consciousness. Recounting the great impact Yogananda leaves on the West during his stay in Hawaii, the author writes:

> The young people vying with each other to pull the Great Society to its knees. They denounced its morbid money culture listing the types of rottenness in that cesspool. They grieved at a national calamity – monstrous crimes – made tenfold more heinous by being placidly accepted as a habit. Permissive in a different context they said mockfully, bitter in their over-reaction. And they

> flung spears at the self-created Frankenstein as it stalked the American continent (181-82)

Though mainly set in the background of the island of Hawaii, the novel also records how India of the late seventies faces an acute energy-crisis – power shortage and oil-crisis:

> Indian economy was hit hard by power shortage and the fuel resources in the country were severely strained. Nuclear power seemed the only answer. But the question of safety was involved, uncontrolled radioactivity could bring about disaster. (149)

Describing the setback received by the economy of the poor and developing countries owing to oil-crisis, the author writes:

> the explosion of hunger was not of India's making. The country's economy was gaining strength and the success of the Green Revolution could settle the problem of food for a long time. But all at once History struck this economy with a sword-thrust. History in the person of the Arabs. The Arabs with their oil and their economic imperialism were feeding on the lifeblood of the poor nations of Asia and Africa, for whom they could have had some human compassion. Take India's case. It would be no exaggeration to say that India's economic future was being decided in the Mid-East deserts floating on an ocean of oil. (196)

Bhabani Bhattacharya reflects the modern Indian social scene not only in his novels, but also in his short-stories. Some of the most memorable stories in the anthology, *Steel Hawk and Other Stories*, deal with the problems of destitution and crime prompted by desperate poverty. With his scathing irony, he exposes in these stories social evils which thwart India's effort to move in the direction of progress and development.

"Glory at Twilight," the opening story of his collection, brings to light the malpractices of the callous money-lenders. The exploitation of the poor villagers by the "sharks" even in the independent India makes Shrinath doubt if India can ever make real progress:

> Where will our India be if such things are tolerated? What is Nehru doing about it? Is there no one to tell him how things stand in the country?[13]

Bhattacharya also deals with the problems of dowry system, one of the greatest curses of the Indian society. He feels that dowry is the root cause of the disharmony in the marital relations in India. The misery of a poor father who is unable to raise adequate dowry for the marriage of his daughter finds expression through Shrinath:

> His face saddened, "What is to be done?" he moaned. "The groom's father is a man of stone. He will break off the marriage unless cash is paid to him before the ceremony starts. Who will ever marry Beena, after such dishonour?" (22)

In the next story, "Public Figure," Bhattacharya ridicules the mean and petty-minded political leaders whose mushroom growth spells out disaster to the country. The cycle of destitution – starvation – death which is the characteristic core of Bhattacharya's novels, is also the theme of "A Moment of Eternity." It is the pathetic tale of a woman who, consequent upon her husband's death brought about by poverty, worry and disease, is driven to such despair that she kills her two children and attempts to commit suicide. In "My Brave Great-Uncle" and "The Quack," the writer portrays the superstitious old man and the wayside quack, suggesting that orthodoxy, superstitions, quackery and ignorance still dominate the present-day society in India. In the title story, "Steel Hawk," Bhattacharya reflects the gradual change of the rural society which has been earlier manacled by rigidity, orthodoxy, superstition and ignorance. It warmly greets the approaching dawn – the Age of machine. Bhattacharya suggests in this story that the spirit of the times – the zest for progress and rapid industrialization – influences even the tradition-ridden old persons like Grandma. Bhattacharya's stories are thus characterized by the same social purpose as permeates his novels.

Bhabani Bhattacharya is a novelist with a vision – the vision of a new India. In all his novels and short stories, he is mainly concerned with the future of his country, its social and religious, economic and political regeneration so that it may make rapid progress and attain its pride of place in the comity of the world's highly developed nations. He does not bring to focus the personal relations among his characters. The communion among them exists purely on social, religious, economic and political level. The dominant motif of his novels is to usher in a new social order in India, based on justice, equality, cooperation and the judicious synthesis of the old and the modern. It is this broad humanitarian vision of life projected through his works that has made Bhattacharya a writer of great relevance and significance.

NOTES

1. Sudhakar Joshi, "An Evening with Bhabani," *The Sunday Standard*, April 24, 1969, p. vii.
2. Dorothy Blair Shimer, "Bhabani Bhattacharya Gandhi Biographer,"*The Journal of Indian Writing in English*, II, ii (July 1974), pp. 15-16.
3. Bhabani Bhattacharya, *Gandhi the Writer: The Image as it Grew* (New Delhi: National Book Trust, 1969), pp. 228-29.
4. Lila Ray, "Bhabani Bhattacharya: A Profile," *Indian Literature*, XI, 2, (April-July 1968), p. 74.
5. *Ibid.*, p. 75.
6. K.R.Chandrasekharan, *Bhabani Bhattacharya* (New Delhi: Arnold Heinemann, 1974), p. XV
7. Bhabani Bhattacharya, *So Many Hungers* (Bombay: Jaico, 1974), p. 65.
8. Bhabani Bhattacharya, *Music for Mohini* (New Delhi: Orient Paperbacks, 1952), p. 67.
9. Bhabani Bhattacharya, *He Who Rides a Tiger* (Delhi: Hind Pocket Books, 1954), p. 18.
10. Bhabani Bhattacharya, *A Goddess Named Gold* (Delhi: Hind Pocket Books, 1960), p. 7.
11. Bhabani Bhattacharya, *Shadow from Ladakh* (Delhi. Hind Pocket Books, 1968), p. 31.
12. Bhabani Bhattacharya, *A Dream in Hawaii* (Madras: Macmillan, 1978), p. 72.
13. Bhabani Bhattacharya, *Steel Hawk and Other Stories* (Delhi: Hind Pocket Books, 1968), p. 22.

Bhattacharya's Concept of Fiction

Every creative artist has his own views about the technique and function of the genre he practises. It is natural for him to follow these principles pertaining to the techniques in his own creative work. Bhabani Bhattacharya, too, like many of his predecessors and contemporary men of letters, has his definite views on literature in general and the novel in particular. From time to time, he has discussed these principles of the craft of fiction elaborately. He vehemently pleads for the depiction of reality in literature. According to him, a creative writer must record the life around him truthfully, though artistically:

> the creative writer's final business is to reveal the truth. He reveals it, unlike the philosopher, in no cold statements of dogma but only in terms of life, rendered through the devices of dramatization.[1]

Though pointedly expressed, the author's contention is not altogether new or unorthodox. In fact, he is simply highlighting the new trends of the novel. The advent of the nineteenth century had already marked the development of realistic fiction. Munshi Premchand, Saratchandra Chatterjee and Rabindranath Tagore were the great exponents of realism in Hindi and Bengali fiction. Inspired by these "great" masters and influenced by the spirit of the times, Bhattacharya too, like Mulk Raj Anand and R.K. Narayan, depicts life realistically in his novels and short-stories. But realism in Bhattacharya's case is essentially a social one. For him, the fiction has to manifest a social purpose. In an interview he observes: "I hold that a novel must have a social purpose. It must place before the reader something from the society's point-of-view.[2]

This, however, does not mean that Bhattacharya negates the presence of the romantic or the imaginative strain along with the modern realistic one. He admits: "There are masters of realism as also those treading in the footprints of the masters. But a great mass of writing, readable, technically superb, shows the deceptive face of the 'real' without the true spirit."[3] He differs with those who think that modern literature is full of realism alone. He maintains that the change has been not so much in the subject-matter as in the ways and methods of its presentation:

> The change on the whole is more in the form than in the basic content. Cindrella continues to have her wonder nights. The Prince of Grandma's fairy tale still tries to create a thrill or a heart throb. There is a difference in the setting. The old simplicity that was the essential charm of the fairy tale has been lost in a labyrinth of motives, a complex of reactions. There is a new intellectualism, but it is only a veneer.[4]

Bhattacharya rejects the idea of "art for art's sake" outright. He considers this theory as odd and funny as to raise the slogans of "science for the sake of science."[5] According to him,

> Art is not necessarily for art's sake. Purposeless art and literature which is much in vogue does not appear to me a sound judgement.[6]

Bhattacharya's views in this respect are similar to Premchand's who also judges art by virtue of its utility and thinks that modern literature "is not a thing merely for entertainment, it has a specific purpose, too. It does not now-a-days relate the meeting-separation story of the hero and the heroine, but also deals with the problems of life and provides their solutions."[7] Mulk Raj Anand, too, denounces such a writer as thinks that he is not interested in *la condition humaine.* He does not attach any weight to the idea of art for art's sake. In his view, neither the West nor the East could adopt the doctrine of pure art – the art that gave delight only and only to the readers.[8]

R.K.Narayan is an objective artist. He does not consider the novel to be a vehicle for the author's views and prejudices. "Readability"[9] – the inherent quality to hold the reader's interest from the very first page to the last – is the only attribute that he considers above all the other merits of a good novel. He warns the readers not to seek moral lessons in his works:

> They always try to read meaning into my books, trace a theme, relate this character to that, make a connection between hero and hero. I wish they would leave me and my books alone.[10]

Bhattacharya's faith in the efficacy of the creative art with a purpose is so firm that he records faithfully all the changing facets of Indian society from 1940 onwards to the late seventies in his fiction. Seen in the perspective of the epoch-making events of Indian history, his works, therefore, constitute a social document of great value.

Maintaining that art must be for life's sake, Bhattacharya also opines that literature, particularly the creative literature, should be instructive to humanity. He believes that there should be a fusion of the ethical values in literature. But these values must be presented in such a way that the creative art expressing them does not become merely didactic, imposing moral codes of conduct upon its readers, nor does it appear to be superfluous portrayal of the reality of social life. He thinks that if a work of creative writing with a plea for moral values is labelled *propaganda literature*, the writer has no reason to be upset about it. He observes:

> Art must teach but unobtrusively, by its vivid interpretation of life. Art must preach, but only by virtue of its being a vehicle of truth. If that is propaganda, there is no need to eschew the world.[11]

Bhattacharya also ridicules the idea of a writer with a moral purpose being termed *tendentious*. He believes that such a writer is usually an idealist who seeks to preach higher moral values for humanity through his writings. In his opinion, the so-called tendentious writer may well be reckoned a good creative artist provided that he depicts life realistically.[12]

Thus, in a way Bhattacharya defends a "committed" writer like Mulk Raj Anand who not only vividly portrays in his fiction the life of Indian untouchables, coolies or bonded labourers—the under-dogs of society—but also vehemently appeals for their uplift.[13] This is why Steinbeck's *The Grapes of Wrath* (1939), dealing with misery and plight of the Okies, and raising a strong voice in protest against the social injustice and demanding a fair deal in society, appealed to Bhattacharya a great deal. Though not basically a committed writer himself, Bhattacharya still has his axes to grind and, as such, he has taken keen interest in analyzing the social conditions, political upheavals and economic problems of his people in his fiction.

Bhattacharya argues that a true creative writer, and particularly a novelist, should deal with the themes related to humanity and its problems. Creative art is to be linked more with human life than nature. He remarks:

> How could values in art help getting involved in the values of human living? . . . he (the novelist) has his deep roots in his fellow-beings. It is they, not nature, who give him his creative fire. Poetry may still depend on nature, though modern poetry increasingly ceases to do so. The novel and the drama, the two forms of creative art that have almost replaced the epic and the lyric, are wholly concerned with the human scenes.[14]

Mulk Raj Anand also agrees with Bhattacharya insofar as the significance of "values of art" is concerned. He, too, avers:

> The destiny of man has been the subject of poetry from the epics downwards. Contemporary writing cannot escape from the motive power of questions like death, love, hatred, greed, avarice, etc. From this point of view, all our artistic works say something, implying value judgements at the back of the mind of the writers.[15]

There is, however, a marked difference in their approach to the treatment of life in art. Unlike Bhattacharya who reckons the novel a creative art dealing with social reality, Anand considers it as "the weapon of humanism."[16] Bhattacharya contends that even while writing about personal relationship or love, a sincere novelist depicts the social reality in his works:

> "I shall write a story of love, just love," the novelist of today may tell himself, and one of the two things will happen to him. If he is intellectually honest somewhere in the course of his narration he will find himself caught in the meshes of reality. For love cannot exist in a vacuum.[17]

He observes that there is no ivory-tower living for a true novelist. He cannot afford to deal with the themes related to romantic escapism – the products of pure imagination, lacking human interest. The novelist "reveals the truth" and takes this task as his "final business." Munshi Premchand expresses similar ideas when he says: "No doubt, a writer with a deep understanding of human nature can express the realities of life even in the love-stories of the old princess and miracle tales, and thus create Beauty. But this also implies the fact that in order to make a literature impressive it must be a mirror to the realities of life. Then you can fit it in whatever frame you wish – even the story of a sparrow and that of a nightingale may be fit for it."[18]

Since according to Bhattacharya the novelist has to record the truth of the social life of the times he is dealing with, he has to be keenly observant and discerning. Bhattacharya himself observes the things around him minutely, and then records his impressions sincerely. Emphasizing the quality of keen perception in a writer, he remarks:

> Unless a writer has keen observation and an eye for noting the details of general behaviour of folks, he cannot write a social novel. I have developed this habit and I have not missed a single opportunity of observing incidents, happenings, where I can gain something for my writer in me. Most of my characters have shaped themselves from the real earth.[19]

Bhattacharya rejects the view that the novelist should not deal with the current events and the prevailing conditions of social life in his fiction simply because he lacks the necessary objectivity and distance to understand and analyze them fully. He is of the view that the current happenings and incidents in the society alone can provide the novelist with necessary material to work upon. In his opinion a creative writer is more sensitive to the things happening around him than common man, and as he has the power of "keen observation" with an "eye for noting the details" of people's ways and activities, he can successfully delineate the existing social reality of his times. He elaborates this idea by pointing out that a novelist is impelled by his creative urge to write. Whenever that creative urge is set afire by the current happenings of the day, the novelist creates a new work of fiction. He observes:

> It has been argued that the novelist should not draw his material from contemporary reality, since he is too close to it to be able to read its meaning and assess its inward nature. This is absurd. The creative writer has a well-developed sensitivity, though this does not mean that he understands or shares all emotions. The things he witnesses, the things he experiences are likely to move him more intensely than what may be called re-collection at second hand. Even the historical novel relies as much on the writer's

> personal experience as on imaginative evocation. Tolstoy's *War and Peace* is a good example. . . . A second point is that true novelist writes because he must. If the events of today have moved him so deeply that he must have a creative outlet for his feelings, why should he put those feelings in cold storage, as it were, and leave them there until the present time has slipped into the vistas of dim yesterdays.[20]

Bhattacharya's conviction regarding the suitability of the contemporary social or historical events as the subject matter proper for the novel, is also evident in his suggestion that "our own history of today is fit material for a novelist. That history need not wait for fifty years before it is declared suitable for fictional projection."[21]

Though no one will dispute Bhattacharya's emphasis on keen discerning power, acute sensitivity and creative urge as the essential attributes of a good novelist, his views regarding the effectiveness of the "contemporary reality" or "the events of today" as the suitable themes in the novel are to be treated as his personal preferences rather than generalizations. It is true that contemporary history as the theme of fiction has held a special fascination for several Indian English novelists like K.S. Venkataramani who treats the "Salt Satyagraha" movement of 1930 in his *Kandan the Patriot*(1932) or Khwaja Ahmed Abbas who in his novel *Inquilab* (1955) traces the history of India from the *Khilafat* movement upto the Gandhi-Irwin Pact, or Khushwant Singh who records the woeful tale of India's partition in *Train to Pakistan* (1956). There are, however, many novelists who have deliberately avoided the treatment of political problems in their works. In none of his novels R.K. Narayan deals with the problems of contemporary India. Even in *Waiting for Mahatma* which portrays the character and personality of Mahatma Gandhi, he shows the great Indian leader in relation to ordinary events of life rather than stirring political events of the period. "At a time when the country was pre-occupied with getting rid of the British, he wrote his stories as if Malgudi was the centre of the universe, and the domestic occurrences in a middle class family to the extent they impinged on a schoolboy or an undergraduate were all that mattered."[22]

With the exception of *Kanthapura* (1938), no other novel of Raja Rao treats of the socio-political situation in modern India. He considers novel as "Sastra" and communicates through it his metaphysical ideas.[23] The other three novels of Raja Rao viz., *The Serpent and the Rope* (1960), *The Cat and Shakespeare* (1965) and *Comrade Kirillov* (1976), are more of treatises in metaphysics than novels.[24]

A novelist who deals with the contemporary life in his fiction may appear journalistic in his approach, but in fact, it is not so. According to Bhattacharya, a creative artist writes spontaneously, covering the naked reality with an artistic touch, whereas a journalist has to write conscious and calculated reports of the incidents and occurrences.

Contrary to C. Paul Verghese's contention that the transmutation of the recent events into the fiction necessarily takes time and that a novelist recording the current happenings in his novels is more apt to be journalistic,[25] Bhattacharya holds that journalistic writing is neither spontaneous nor a result of any inner urge, whereas a true creative work of fiction essentially has both these qualities. He observes:

> The idea prevails in some strength that a novel may be contemporary in the sense that it deals with our immediate yesterdays. But not today, not the current hour, the current moment. But why not? It is said that fictional work will then drop to the level of journalism. It will be a kind of reporting. With this point of view I do not agree. A journalist does not need spontaneity. He does not write because he must. The creative artist on the contrary, has a compulsion to find an outlet for the living images in him. So I say: A novelist may well be concerned with today, the current hour or moment, if it is meaningful for him, if it moves him sufficiently into emotional response. An instance that comes to my mind among a score of others is Steinbeck's *The Grapes of Wrath.* That great book, depicting an immediate and acute problem of the time of its writing, could easily have become brilliant journalism. Instead, it became a true piece of fiction.[26]

Bhattacharya thinks that a novelist should portray his people's aspirations and struggles to attain better social, political and economic life-conditions. According to him, "it will be appropriate for a novelist of today to make the spiritual values of our Five Year Plans the basis of his theme. Those spiritual values expressed through living images, creatures of flesh and blood and feeling, may well give a new direction to our creative endeavour."[27]

Bhattacharya is of the view that Indian writers of the present generation, though fortunate enough to witness the turning-points of the national life, have either failed to depict them effectively in their fiction, or lacked the strong creative urge to write about them. He remarks:

> War has washed our borders and the effect has been felt all over the subcontinent. The struggle for freedom has rocked the land. Famine of a kind conceivable only to a Dante's imagination has actually taken place. The tragedies of partition have been beyond anything that a writer could "invent." But where is the creative expression of all these happenings?

He does not agree with the argument that the current social conditions or the historical events often befuddle the modern Indian novelist emotionally, leaving him confused and incapable of converting the fact into fiction. Nor does he hold the novelist's lack of the required awareness of the historical events a deterrent factor. In his opinion, it is the narrow aesthetics of a writer which discourages him from reflecting the contemporary problems in his works rather than his limited knowledge of political events:

> It would not be true to say that our writers lack the necessary awareness. Certain aesthetic conceptions, it seems to me, have been the deterrent. Indian writing has suffered from these false conceptions in a greater measure than is generally realized. The fields of art have lain fallow in the farther reaches beyond the limited range of mental horizons.[29]

Mulk Raj Anand, who has portrayed the contemporary problems in his novels, is also of the view that anything could make a novel provided one kept in view the limitations of the form, that is to say, confined it to human beings – their relations with each other, in the warp and woof of the time in which they live, conceived through the imagination or transformed by it.

In Hindi, Munshi Premchand frequently drew his themes from the prevailing social conditions and political events of his times. Almost all his novels and stories deal with the contemporary realities. He was the first Indian novelist to take the material for his novels and stories from the contemporary life and present it artistically in a living language and artistic style. Instead of writing books merely after reading books, he got the theme of his stories from the contemporary socio-political movements, his personal life and the people around him.

For Bhattacharya, a writer can project a true image of his country and its ethos only when he deals with the problems of his times in his writings. He holds:

> It is not often that a novelist is fortunate enough to live at a turning-point of national life. The turning-point faces us with its challenge. Will not some of India's novelists accept the challenge? I hope the response will come from writers in the English sector, in particular, for they would then be revealing the new Indian dream to vast audiences the world over.[30]

Bhattacharya is not averse to the depiction of sex in the novel. Sex can be a powerful subject-matter for fiction since it constitutes an integral part of human life. There should not be any impositions or restraints regarding sex in literature. Since the novel as a creative art is finally concerned with the "human scene," sex as a theme cannot be omitted as its omission will limit the vision of the novelist whose "final business" is to reveal the "truth" of life in a realistic way. Bhattacharya declares:

> I am not one for tabooing sex in literature. I don't believe in censorship. And I welcome good literature where sex is symbolically suggested. It is an inevitable part of human life and I believe, it has its place in literature too.[31]

He, however, pleads for a suggestive and meaningful treatment of the sex-theme in the novel so that it acquires artistic touch about it. A naked pornography is not art in any sense for him. He despises sensuality as a cheap device for entertainment and asks for the beautification and sublimation of the passions in the novels:

> can we not beautify it (sex in literature) instead? The flow of cheap paperback, vulgar, low-taste books revelling in sex description cannot be welcome. I have a revulsion for them. But look at Lawrence. He creates a whole world of this much tabooed feeling and yet the descriptions are most beautiful and excel in their

lyrical quality. Look at Hemingway and you will learn how sex can be a theme to write upon, without making it repulsive.[32]

Bhattacharya ridicules the so-called romantic writers who indulge in vulgar and pornographic descriptions of the sexual revelries of their heroes and heroines with a view to making them appear real to life. He does not consider such novelists mature and true artists:

> The so-called romantic writer of today seems to woo actuality by depicting in detail and with sharp photographic accuracy the sex convolutions of his Cindrella and his Prince, thus giving them roots apparently in the common earth of life and time. Here is an adolescent determined to be an adult.[33]

His opinion about the significance of the artistic treatment of sex in fiction notwithstanding, Bhattacharya generally avoids it in his own novels. Though stray references of rape – actual (*So Many Hungers)* or attempted (*He Who Rides a Tiger*), – and of love – pure (*A Goddess Named Gold)* or passionate (*Shadow from Ladakh)* and *A Dream in Hawaii)* – are present in his novels, yet the novelist does not describe it in detail and with sharp photographic accuracy in his fiction. In this respect Bhattacharya is close to R.K.Narayan who does not exploit perversion or sex as a theme in his fiction. In fact, Narayan's attitude towards sex is the conventional, mid-Victorian attitude. He avoids the portrayal of the scenes dramatizing physical passions in his novels. Even the infatuation between the young Raju and the romantic Rosie is conveyed in *The Guide* by covert suggestions.

Premchand's attitude towards sex and man-woman relationship is conventional. He does not appreciate the notions of free sex, and there are numerous instances in his fiction when he ridicules flirtation – the so-called modern sexual liberty. Sex for Premchand is permissible only within marital life. The respect for the female dignity and high moral character are the main concern in his novels and stories. He does not like to see man-woman relationship defiled or debased. Though Bhattacharya recognizes the potentiality of the sex-themes in the novel, yet he does not appreciate its licentious treatment in Sasthi Brata's novels. The latter novelist frequently indulges in the brutally frank details of love-making instead of treating it in a subtle and suggestive way.[34]

Bhattacharya has not broken any new grounds so far as the technique of fiction is concerned. As a craftsman he is more of a traditionalist than an experimentalist. Yet he is not altogether averse to the new modes or techniques of fiction. Sudhaker Joshi remarks that although Bhattacharya "writes fairly objectively, he does not look down upon the new techniques and trends in prose writing."[35] Bhattacharya does not suggest any particular style or technique of writing to other novelists because he is of the view:

> A writer chooses a style that suits his theme and genius most. Personally, I have always felt like writing in a way I write now. I cannot give my opinion on Narayan or Malgonkar since it is for them to decide what way they should write.[36]

The stream-of-consciousness technique, which has found favour with many modern writers, does not interest him. He, however, does not denounce it. To him, it is simply an experiment in the mode of writing novels: a mere swing of pendulum which is natural in the process of maturity and perfection of the style of creative writing. Although the present-day modes of expression are not the perfect ones in his opinion, yet he is optimistic that a balanced technique of fiction-writing will be evolved in near future.[37]

The stream-of-consciousness technique seeks to record the random and apparently illogical flow of impressions passing through a character's mind. Dorothy Richardson, Virginia Woolf and James Joyce who rejected the socio-descriptive novel used this technique to focus their attention on the character itself. Since Bhattacharya is interested more in treating socio-economic problems of contemporary India than in analyzing the human pysche, he does not much employ this technique in his fiction, though he is quite capable of handling it effectively, some striking instances of which can be found in his latter novels and especially in *A Dream in Hawaii*. On the contrary, Anand, who is interested in presenting a vivid picture of the workings of human mind, makes a frequent use of it in his novels. He states:

> In London, when I worked as an assistant in the rare book shop of Jacob Schwarts, I read Joyce's *Portrait of the Artist as a Young Man, Ulysses* and parts of *Work in Progress*. The "stream-of-consciousness" method of James Joyce swept me off my feet. I felt that

> the application of this technique to the labyrinths and substrata of Indian mind could alone metamorphose the inner realities of soul.[38]

Anand's *Untouchable* (1935) gives perhaps the best illustration of the use of the stream-of-consciousness technique, and the reader is moved by Bakha's broodings, inner conflicts and silent reaction to what happens around him. Anand has himself admitted that he "seeks to absorb the stream-of-consciousness method of James Joyce, especially in *Untouchable*."[39]

As regards the language of the novelist, Bhattacharya pleads for a full freedom of the choice.[40] A writer can choose any medium of expression that suits his genius most and through which he can communicate himself with ease and felicity. He himself likes to write in English because, as he remarks:

> I have loved writing in English. The creative writer must have full freedom to use the language of his choice. If he decides on a foreign tongue, he will have to cross immense technical hurdles, but that is his headache. I have enjoyed the challenge of this literary problem – expressing Indian life in the medium of an alien language.[41]

He considered English to be "a bridge that carries our cultural values to the world – not only to the English-speaking countries but to most of the other countries as well, in translation."[42]

R.K.Narayan too has chosen English as the medium of expression in his fiction because he can express himself better through it than through any other language. He does not consider English a foreign language, but holds that India's long association with English and the English has mitigated the sense of alienness towards this language. On being asked by William Walsh whether he felt any strain while writing in "another" language, Narayan replied:

> Until you mentioned your tongue I never had any idea that I was writing in another tongue. My whole education has been in English from the primary school, and most of my reading has been in the English language. The language and literature of this country flourished in the Indian soil until lately. It still remains the language of the intelligentsia. But English has been with us for

> over a century and a half. I am particularly fond of the language. I was never aware that I was using a different, a foreign language when I wrote in English because it came to me very easily. I can't explain how. English is a very adaptable language. And so transparent it can take on the tint of any country.[43]

Mulk Raj Anand too, like Bhattacharya reckons English as "a bridge" carrying Indian cultural values to the West. He says that he wrote in English because it was

> the only language that came to hand in a difficult transitional period. And we wanted to say or say immediately, notwithstanding the political and moral censorship that inhibited our languages.... And ... our writing in English is ... a part of the Indian cultural development and has its values, if only as an interpretative literature of the most vital character.[44]

Anand is, however, one of those Indian English novelists who consciously strive to adapt English to suit their purpose. He is of the view that English cannot adequately express Indian ethos till it uses freely idioms and metaphors of the Indian languages. An Indian writer has to evolve his own kind of Indian English to convey Indian sentiments successfully. Anand does so by literally translating dialogues in his novels from his mother-tongue, Punjabi. He confesses:

> I found, while writing spontaneously, that I was always translating dialogue from the original Punjabi into English. The way in which my mother said something in a dialect of central Punjab could not have been expressed in any other way except in an almost literal translation, which might carry over the sound and sense of the original speech. . . . This self-analysis enabled me to consciously introduce translation of Punjabi, Urdu and Hindi words into all my writings.[45]

Raja Rao is another Indian English writer who, faced by the dilemma of conveying Indian sentiments through the English language, adapts it to his own kind of Indian English rich in the idiom and regional speech of Kannada-speaking people in South India. Since an Indian, according to him, cannot write like an Englishman because of his peculiar environment, the language of the Indo-English writer is bound to have a distinct character of its own. Raja Rao refers to this type of English used by Indians when in the "Preface" of *Kanthapura*, he remarks:

> The telling has not been easy. One has to convey in a language that is not one's own the spirit that is one's own. One has to convey the various shades and omissions of a certain thought-movement that looks mal-treated in an alien language. I use the word "alien," yet English is not really an alien language to us. It is the language of our intellectual make up – like Sanskrit or Persian was before – but not of our emotional make up. We are all instinctively bilingual, many of us writing in our own language and in English. We cannot write like the English. We should not. We cannot write only as Indians. We have grown to look at the large world as part of us. Our method of expression therefore has to be a dialect which will some day prove to be as distinctive and colourful as the Irish or the American. Time alone will justify it.[46]

According to Bhattacharya, a creative artist can write only when he feels a strong creative urge. Writing for the sake of writing has no meaning for him. Whenever he feels his creative urge, the theme in his subconscious mind starts taking the shape of a story, and he has simply to put it down on paper. There is a spontaneous development of the story or characters in his case. He observes in this connection:

> I have not believed in writing for the sake of writing. I seldom planned a story structure. Each story grew in my subconscious mind as it were. When it had grown enough, I had to give it physical form. The characters even when I had decided how they are going to behave moved by their own volition, often defeating my purpose.[47]

He is of the opinion that it is not always possible for the novelist to know the course his story is going to take during the process of its development. In his own case, for instance, impelled by the natural urge to create, he takes up a particular theme, invents characters and incidents, gives them definite shape, and starts assigning them appropriate roles in the narrative. But their growth is spontaneous and independent of the creator's will. Speaking of his method of work, Bhattacharya observes:

> When I feel like writing upon a theme, and the characters and events fit in the pattern, I start putting it down on paper. But, once I start writing, it is not I, but the characters and situations that compel me to be led by them. It is they who should decide the way they should end. The end of the story, in my case, is never the one which I had in my mind in the beginning. Even the original plan itself gets modified or changed due to certain traits, which my characters develop during the course of events. It will be therefore a violence if I stick to my original plan while the characters change.[48]

As a matter of fact, the technique in a work of art varies from artist to artist. It is a subjective matter. Like Bhattacharya, Premchand also takes up a theme and knits the web of a story around it. Though both invent characters to fit in the pattern of their stories, yet in Bhattacharya's case the characters develop spontaneously and independently, often deviating from the writer's original intention, whereas in Premchand's case, they remain under the tight grip of the author, and cannot move "by their own volition." While the former is primarily interested in choosing his theme from the contemporary events and incidents, the latter finds a suitable theme even in the history of remote past. Premchand's reply to the query as to how he wrote his stories, is significant:

> My stories are often based on some or the other inspiration or experience to which I try to give a dramatic colouring. But I do not write stories simply in order to narrate an incident, I wish to illustrate some philosophical and emotional truths in it. I cannot write until there is such a base. On finding one, I invent characters. Sometimes History also provides with plots. But any incident is not a story unless it expresses some psychological fact. I do not start writing until I set a story in my mind from its beginning to the end. I create the characters with a view that they suit that story. I do not think it necessary at all to base my story on some interesting incident. Provided that a story has a psychological climax, be it related to any incident then, I care a fig.[49]

R.K. Narayan's technique, in this respect, is different from that of Bhattacharya and Premchand. While the latter chooses themes that strike their respective minds and thereafter weave the patterns of their stories, inventing characters and events which are integral to the plot, R.K. Narayan lays greater emphasis on character instead of the plots of his novels. Once he himself stated that he "started a book on being provided by an odd or eccentric character."[50] Though his earlier novels, being more or less autobiographical, contain the characters which are mostly drawn from his personal acquaintances, yet from *Mr. Sampath* (1949) onwards, Narayan generally invents them and "it would seem that the starting point is not a plot but a character, in every sense of that latter term."[51] Out of the oddities and eccentricities of his characters emerge Narayan's stories, but during the course of the development of plot, the writer loses his hold upon the characters and they "often wander off on their own."[52]

A novelist, according to Bhattacharya, must have full freedom in the choice both of the medium of expression and the subject-matter of the novel. The style and technique, the methods of expression, should also be of his choice. He must have the power of "keen observation" to discern the details of life around him. He should depict "truth" of the life as he sees it, though artistically, "through the devices of dramatization." A novel, in Bhattacharya's sense of the term, should be written with a "social purpose" in view, and should portray a picture of the society the novelist lives in. A novelist who has "well-developed sensitivity" can transform the contemporary events into an artistic work of fiction if they set his imagination afire and impel him to create.

All the novels by Bhattacharya uphold his concept of fiction and amply illustrate how he delineates the social realities of the contemporary times truthfully and artistically with the help of his sharp sensitivity and keenly discerning power. He portrays in his fiction, as has been shown in the preceding chapter, the modern Indian society in its multifarious aspects.

NOTES

1. Bhabani Bhattacharya, "Literature and Social Reality," *The Aryan Path,* XXVI, ix (September 1955), p. 395.
2. Sudhakar Joshi, p.vii.
3. "Literature and Social Reality," p. 395.
4. *Ibid.*, p. 392.

5. *Ibid.*, p. 394. Bhattacharya avers here: "Could it be that the fairy-tale genre of writing, still drew its zest from the muffled cry of 'art for art's sake?' I say muffled, since there has been a realization that 'art for art's sake' is as queer a demand as, say, science for the sake of science. Could the arms, face and the liver of a man claim autonomy in the same manner, just because each performed a definite function of its own?"
6. Sudhakar Joshi, p. vii.
7. Hansraj Rahbar, *Prem Chand: Jiwan, Kala aur Krititva* (Delhi: Atma Ram, 1962), p. 311.
8. M.K.Naik, *Mulk Raj Anand* (New Delhi: Arnold-Heinemann India, 1973), pp. 175-76.
9. P.S. Sundaram, *R.K.Narayan* (New Delhi: Arnold-Heinemann India, 1973), p. 141.
10. Ved Mehta, *John is Easy to Please*, pp. 150-51, quoted by Sundaram in *R.K.Narayan*, p. 15.
11. "Literature and Social Reality," p. 395.
12. *Loc. cit.*
13. All the novels by Anand, and especially *Untouchable* (1935), *Coolie* (1936) and *Two leaves and a Bud* (1937), champion the cause of the downtrodden.
14. "Literature and Social Reality," p. 394.
15. Anand's reply to Naik's questionnaire, quoted in *Mulk Raj Anand*, p. 175.
16. Mulk Raj Anand, "Old Myths and New Myths: Recital versus Novel," *The Banasthali Patrika*, XIII, July 1969, p. 35.
17. "Literature and Social Reality," p. 394.
18. Hansraj Rahbar, p. 310.
19. Sudhakar Joshi, p. vii.
20. "Literature and Social Reality," pp. 395-96.
21. Bhabani Bhattacharya, "Indo-Anglian," *The Novel in Modern India*, ed. Iqbal Bakhtiyar (Bombay: The P.E.N. All-India Centre, 1964), p. 47.
22. P.S. Sundaram, p. 139.
23. David McCutchion, "The Novel as Sastra," *Considerations*, ed. Meenakshi Mukherjee (New Delhi: Allied, 1977), pp 99-101
24. Anand's observation about Raja Rao's fiction is plausible. He notes: After the first novel, however, he (Raja Rao) becomes an anti-novel novelist self-consciously using the philosophical essay as part of the bardic recital form. The reflections on moral importances begin to weigh on the novel. *The Banasthali Patrika*, XIII, p. 35.
25. C. Paul Verghese, "The Problem of the Indian Novelist in English," *The Banasthali Patrika*, No. XII (January 1969), p. 87.
26. "Indo-Anglian," p. 47.
27. *Loc. cit.*
28. "Literature and Social Reality," p. 396.
29. *Loc. cit.*
30. "Indo-Anglian," pp. 47-48.
31. Sudhakar Joshi, p. vii.
32. *Loc. cit.*
33. "Literature and Social Reality," p. 392.

34. Sasthi Brata's *She and He* (Orient Paperbacks, 1973) amply illustrates the sexual revelries of its male and female characters without any moral scruples or inhibitions. But for some reflective passages found here and there, the novel verges on pornographic writing.
35. Sudhakar Joshi, p. vii.
36. *Loc. cit.*
37. *Loc. cit.*
38. M.K. Naik, p. 20.
39. Anand, "Old Myths and New Myths: Recital versus Novel," p. 35.
40. "Indo-Anglian," pp. 42-43. Bhattacharya speaks of the fundamental right of a creative writer to express his views in the medium of his liking.
41. Chandrasekharan, pp. 2-3. Quoted from *Contemporary Novelists in the English Language* (New York: St. Martin's Press, 1972), p. 38.
42. "Indo-Anglian," p. 42.
43. B.B.C. Third Programme, Feb. 22, 1968, interviewer William Walsh, extracts of the same reproduced by Walsh in his booklet: *R.K. Narayan* (Writers and their Work series, British Council, 1971), p. 7.
44. Mulk Raj Anand, *The King Emperor's English* (Bombay: Kutab Popular, 1948), p. 16.
45. M.K.Naik, p. 163, quoted from Anand's paper, "Pigeon-Indian: Some Notes on Indian-English Writing," presented at a Seminar on Australian and Indian Literature, New Delhi, in 1970.
46. Raja Rao, "Foreword," *Kanthapura* (Delhi: Orient Paperbacks, 1971).
47. Chandrasekharan, p. 2.
48. Sudhakar Joshi, p. vii.
49. Hans Raj Rahbar, p. 323.
50. P.S.Sundaram, p. 62.
51. *Ibid.*, p. 63.
52. Sharda Prasad, "R.K.Narayan, Writer and Novelist," *Traveller in India* (Summer 1969), p. 3.

Tradition and Modernity

Tradition and modernity, like red and white corpuscles in human blood, are antagonistic yet essential components of the flow of life. It is natural, therefore, that their respective meanings, scopes, importance in life, and their clash that provides the creative writing with a major theme, be examined elaborately.

The term, tradition, has very close association with human life and is used with reference to its various aspects. It influences man's personal relationships as well as the collective social life through the spheres of religion, philosophy, culture and literature. Tradition develops with the march of human civilization through advancement or decadence. With the evolution of human history, tradition also grows and faces changes. It has thus been changed, distorted, refined and modulated from time to time, yet it has always maintained its existence. Derived from Latin, the term tradition means:

> A long established and generally accepted custom or method of procedure, having almost the force of a law, an immemorial usage.[1]

Funk & Wagnalls Dictionary describes tradition as "the transmission of knowledge, opinions, doctrines, customs, practices, etc. from generation to generation, originally by word of mouth and by example."[2]

In the literary context specifically, tradition becomes "a body of customs, beliefs, skills or sayings, handed down from generation to generation or age to age. Thus, popular ballads, folktales, and proverbs have been passed down through the centuries by oral tradition, or oral transmission. Tradition, taken from Latin meaning "given through," may be thought of as a body of literary conventions inherited from the past.[3] For example, the tradition of pastoral literature is more than two thousand years old. Robert Frost's poem, "Mending Wall," indicates a New England tradition of repairing stone walls every year. Similarly, Thomas Hardy has depicted the traditional rustic folks with all their characteristics in his famous Wessex novels.

In the general sense of the term, tradition is a continuous process of handing down from generation to generation the conventions, beliefs, habits and even superstitions not only through oral and spontaneous transmission, but also through written, conscious, and selective adoptation of the long-established practice of human society.

The range of tradition is very wide. As a social phenomenon, tradition brings out the sociability in man by insisting on institutionalization, social values and idealizations:

> Tradition, standing for the "processes" of ideas being handed down through succeeding generations, provides the individuals with the background and knowledge of each one of the institutions and facilitates easy incorporation of the ideals and values prevailing in society. . . . The individual being organically related to society draws his inspiration from his society and tradition, by preserving the continuity of ideas of the past with the present supplies the individual with the ideas which have been purified and distilled by the social ethos.[4]

Tradition functions responsibly in regard to the individual as well as the society. It thus steers clear of the anarchic individualism that makes the individual all important and the totalitarianism that destroys the individual and makes the state most supreme.

"History develops, Art stands still,"[5] says E.M. Forster, but this does not imply that traditions in the historical (and of course literary) context and readymade finished phenomena is *just* handed over from one generation to the next, or born out of the human imagination in every generation. In fact, "literary tradition," as Forster observes, "is the borderland lying between literature and history."[6] The technique of laughing at characters has been persistent in the English fiction in every age, though it has changed in its aspects according to the needs and tastes of the respective ages. For instance, the Elizabethan humorist chooses his victim differently from his modern counterpart, and his tricks to make the reading public laugh also vary. Similarly, the technique of fantasy has consistently been prevailing in the English novel, but its practitioners may sometimes differ in its treatment just as Virginia Woolf and Laurence Sterne do.[7]

Tradition is an inclusive term. When studied from the literary point of view particularly, "there can be few areas of literary investigation in which the questions of tradition must not sooner or later be faced,"[8] says S.S. Prawer. In this process, one may also see that in the study of literary tradition the national and the international factors come together in complex ways, and the writers learn from each other even across the linguistic frontiers. For instance, Lermontov takes over from Pushkin the model of the Byronic tales in verse, but he also goes to Byron direct, adopting the features which Pushkin has not introduced into his own "Byron-inspired" tales:

> an author may introduce the influence of a foreign author into a literary tradition, and then, as in the case of the Byronic tradition in Russia, it may proceed largely from the influence of the native author (i.e. Pushkin). But as tradition continues, it may be enriched by another native author (who goes) back to the foreign author for materials or tonalities or images or effects which were not adopted by the first author.[9]

Tradition plays a significant role in the advancement of human knowledge. Being "a perception, not only of the pastness of the past, but of its presence,"[10] tradition is essential even to human existence. S.N. Ganguly throws light on the importance of tradition in human life when he remarks:

> Man built his culture not merely by his tools and toil, but also largely by his indomitable desire to transcend. This urge was fulfilled in his building a world of values over and above the world of facts. With values and ideals in his world-picture, man's problem was not merely to preserve and sustain what he had already achieved but also to shape a future endlessly approximating to his changing ideals. It is only values which make a mere change appear as progress. But all this dreaming activity is grounded in selecting some and rejecting others of his own customs both individually and collectively. Tradition, and this is one of the most important functions, helps man in this selective behaviour. The human potential is realised significantly in a changing world and civilization only through the help of tradition.[11]

But "society being dynamic in character, it necessarily undergoes changes,"[12] and hence, in the process of shaping the course of history, literature, religion, philosophy, etc. of humanity, tradition itself is also modified. Human mind with ever-present reasoning power is prone to question and rationalize the old views and beliefs in every field of life. And this thing causes the change in tradition. The human capacity of assimilation of prevalent ideas and projection of new ideas – the spirit of revolt, reform, restraint and revival – is what paves the way for novelty – for modernity – in human thought and activity.

"The quality or condition of being modern, modernness of character"[13] is what constitutes modernity. In this connection, it is profitable to examine what the term "modern" denotes. *The Oxford English Dictionary* records that "modern" means "of or pertaining to the present and recent times, as distinguished from the remote past; pertaining to or originating in the current age or period.[14] *Funk & Wagnalls Dictionary* notes that the term "modern" signifies "belonging to or characteristic of time not remotely past; not ancient, antiquated, or obsolete, recent."[15]

In the light of these definitions, one may assume that "modernity" is that spirit of newness and uniqueness, be it in the field of literature, art or sculpture, which forces a conscious questioning – a break from the set patterns, established theories and beliefs or all sorts of influences.

Modernity becomes all the more important in the present times. The demand of the age, to cast away all the shackles of convention, to express oneself fully and freely, to be original and innovative in every mode of expression, i.e. art, music, sculpture, or literature, is genuine and strong today. In this respect, Anna Balakian's remark, "what is infinitely more important: the turning point at which the writer frees himself of the influence and finds his originality,"[16] seems equally applicable to the fine arts.

Modernity has an immensely large scope. Every aspect of human civilization falls under its range. With the advancement of man's knowledge, his fields of thoughts and action have also expanded. He started probing deeper into the mysteries of Nature long ago and has succeeded in exploring a great deal by now. The things deemed mysterious, unscrutable and uncontrollable at one time, have remained secret or obscure no more in the course of time. The theories regarded universal and irrevocable in yesterdays are no more applicable today. Actually the "scientific temper of the modern world has made people question the belief considered to be beyond doubt."[17]

The ever-present spirit of questioning and the incessant human thirst for knowledge and more knowledge in every field of life, have forced man either to make a complete break from the past or to mould the old practices and values considerably so as to suit the present-day requirements. Erasmian remarks significantly:

> The new learning asks that every doctrine of supreme importance should be examined afresh and should not, unless it can be proved to demonstration, be proclaimed . . . as eternal truth. And proof is often a very difficult thing.[18]

The tension between tradition and innovation is experienced by every culture and at all times; the nature of the tension may, however, differ according to the historical and social-cultural context.[19] There are two schools of thought – both extremist – one supporting tradition vigorously, and the other refuting it furiously and making a case for modernity strongly. On the one hand, thinkers contend that "adherence to tradition makes the individual unprogressive and inactive and paves the way for the closed society,"[20] on the other hand, it is held that

> in the name of progress, coming under the spell of modernism and being ever-anxious to streamline our ideas to suit the requirements of the "changing situations" we ought not to belittle the value of tradition which after all represents the results of deep thinking that has gone into the problems not dissimilar to those of the present. The very existence of social problems is attributed by this view to the fact that the guiding hand of the wisdom of the past is not accepted.[21]

The idea of progress is based on these two extreme viewpoints:

> The anti-traditionalists would have us believe that man and society can progress only when traditions are thrown away and the traditionalists have a nostalgia to the very idea of progress measured in terms of beginning anew completely.[22]

In literature, too, tradition and modernity have constantly been at loggerheads. The history of English literature may amply reveal to a perceptive reader that this tension has been present from the earliest times to the modern age, though its pitch has not been very high. The dawn of the twentieth century has, however, marked some unusual stirrings in the social, political, economic, cultural and intellectual spheres of life. The industrial revolution and the consequent growth of materialism and self-centredness, resulting in the collapse of the established values and dogmas, and leading finally to the break-out of World War I, have forced the intellectual elite to discard the worn-out and conventional practices in favour of the new and more humane ones:

> Born out of the despair of the world war and civil war, of social unrest and economic chaos, the desire for a complete break with the past, for starting human history from scratch was deep and genuine.[23]

The modern age has, however, not set any clear track for the writer to follow today; rather, it has proved to be an age which has seen some writers reach an ultimate point along the line of bewilderment and disillusion, and others (or indeed, the same ones at another stage or in another phase) making a new start and hammering out the terms of life afresh.

The conflict between tradition and modernity is the result of the East-West encounter experienced by India in the wake of the English rule and the English education. In the complex fabric of contemporary Indian culture, the two easily discerned strands are the indigenous Indian traditions and the modern European conceptions. The East-West encounter highlights the polarities of these two distinct and separate cultures – spiritualism of the East and technological and material values of the West. Almost every educated Indian today is the product of the conflicts and reconciliations of these two cultures, although the consciousness of this tension varies from individual to individual. Focussing on the effect of modernity on educated Indians, Nabneeta Dev Sen remarks:

> The shallow superficial character of modernity, which came to India along with partial modernisation, exerted its complex repercussions on our lives. Our urban elite consists of a motley bunch, often functioning under two contradictory sets of values. He wears a traditional face in domestic life and a modern mask in the public arena. Most of the traditional Indian social institutions like the joint family, or the caste system, even feudalism or serfdom

> still continue under a variety of guises, in spite of the long-standing pressures against them all over India. The values that go with them, therefore, still live within us, while we are trying consciously to adopt modern values from the outside world. There is an external sense of freedom, but an inner feeling of freedomlessness due to his bondage to traditional values acutely bothers the sensitive modern man.[24]

What is generally true of the educated Indian is especially true of the Indian writer because he is more aware than others of the ethos that makes up his personality. A writer's quest for identity involves the evaluation of his own attitude towards the two aspects of his being – one inherited from birth, the other imbibed through education. This cultural conflict has always assumed a vital significance for the Indian novelist who writes in English. His "mixed sensibility" resulting from his intimate understanding of both oriental and occidental values of life gives him a rare advantage as B. Rajan points out, "The presence of two cultures in one's mind forms a wider and therefore a saner basis on which to originate the quest for identity and that the discordance between these cultures can be creative as well as merely confusing."[25] The Indian writer in English is able to view with serenity and objectivity the challenge of contrasting cultures and ways of life.

Sarath Kumar Ghose is the earliest of Indian English writers to deal with the theme of the conflict between tradition and modernity. In his novel, *The Prince of Destiny,* published in 1909, he portrays Barath, the hero of the novel, as the harbinger of the synthesis between East and West, i.e. tradition and modernity. Talking to the people of his state, whose destiny he commands as their ruler, he asks:

> Would you have me be the new Buddha now – or if you will, the new Krishna, not in conquest, but in love? Love for all earth?[26]

At another place when Nova, an English girl, whom he loves dearly, asks him, "what is your mission?," he replies in a confident tone, "To unite East and West, and turn their conflict into concord." (516) In this novel, Vashista, the High Priest of Vishnu and the spiritual mentor of Barath, stands for Indian spiritual values unsullied by any effect of modernism, while Barath and Viswamitra, the retired judge turned ascetic, represent the judicious balance of the traditional and the modern values of life.

India's contact with the Western culture and civilization led to the emergence of three distinct types among educated Indians. There were, on one extreme, fundamentalists who stuck blindly to the old Indian traditions and were sorely averse to the British way of life. On the other extreme were those who had been completely swept off their feet by the English education and who found nothing valuable in their ancient culture and way of life. They were completely anglicized and considered themselves as the epitome of modernity. They look down upon their countrymen as traditionalists and backward. Between these two extremes stood the middle group of judicious people of India who had drawn inspiration from the liberal and democratic values and scientific outlook of the West, and developed broader and cosmopolitan view of life. They were also rooted in their soil and had imbibed the best of the Indian values. They possessed the synthetic view of life and pleaded for the balance of tradition and modernity.

The Indian English novel has given a vivid portrayal of these three different attitudes to this inter-cultural conflict. Vasudev Sastri in B.R. Rajam Iyer's *Vasudev Sastri* (1905), Vashista in S.K. Ghose's *The Prince of Destiny,* Nihal Singh in Mulk Raj Anand's *The Village* (1939) and Mir Nihal in Ahmed Ali's *Twilight in Delhi* (1940), have staunch faith in their traditions. They are full of rancour against the British for introducing new fashions and new ways of life in their country. The parents of Vedantam, Thathachari and Rajamma, in V.V. Chintamani's *Vedantam, The Clash of Traditions* (1938), like the parents of Rama in Hasan Ali's *The Changeling* (1933), are unhappy when their son sails for England to acquire Western education. Steeped deep in Vedic learning, Thathachari has innate hatred for the study of a foreign language and the westernized ways of life. Indian women are shown to be more critical of the modern values than man. Being nourished on Indian traditions and values, Kusum in Nayantara Sahgal's *A Time to be Happy* (1958) finds it difficult to put up with the ways of her westernized husband, Sanad Shivpal. Kamala, the wife of Cambridge-educated Krishnan in B. Rajan's *The Dark Dancer* (1959), and Premala, the wife of anglicized Kitsamy in Kamala Markandaya's *Some Inner Fury* (1957), try to escape from the stifling atmosphere of their homes to find succour in the humanitarian work among the poor people. All of them derive their strength from service and sacrifice, and their unreserved faith in Indian values. In Kamala Markandaya's novel, *A Silence of*

Desire (1961), Sarojini who seeks faith cure for her tumour from a Swami spurns the advice of her husband who asks her to go in for a modern and scientific cure through operation. She tells him:

> Yes, you can call it healing by faith, or healing by the grace of God, if you understand what that means. But I do not expect you to understand – you with your Western notions, your superior talk of ignorance and superstition when all it means is that you don't know, what lies beyond reason and you prefer not to find out.[27]

Kedari in K.S. Venkataramani's *Murugan, the Tiller* (1927), Rangan, the Assistant Collector of Tanjore, in the same author's *Kandan, the Patriot* (1932), Vedantam, the Indian Civil Service Officer in V.V. Chintamani's *Vedantam, The Clash of Tradition*s, Kitsamy, the Oxford-educated District Magistrate in Kamala Markandaya's *Some Inner Fury*, Krishnan whose return to India after his stay in England is described in B. Rajan's *The Dark Dancer*, as "coming back to indifferent sky, an anonymous teeming of houses," and Sanad Shivpal in Nayantara Sahgal's *A Time to be Happy,* belong to the tribe of modernized Indians who find it difficult to understand the traditions and values of Indian life. They are un-Indian in their outlook and fail to identify themselves with the aspirations of their countrymen. Sanad Shivpal describes the predicament of such westernized Indians when he says about himself:

> I don't belong entirely to India, I can't. My education, my upbringing, and my sense of values have all combined to make me an un-Indian.[28]

Ramu in K.S. Venkataramani's *Murugan, the Tiller* and Kandan and Rajeswari Bai in his *Kandan, the Patriot*, reveal a judicious synthesis of the traditional and the modern values of life. Though highly educated, they are not swept off their feet by their English education. They are neither blind followers of the old traditions nor slavish imitators of the modern Western values of life. Raghunath in K. Nagarajan's *Athawar House* (1945) belongs to a conservative Maratha family which adheres to the old traditions blindly. He, however, imbibes modern outlook through his high education and participation in the national movement. He, therefore, does not hesitate to discard outmoded caste and community prejudices and willingly marries his daughter in a Tamil Family.

In Roshan (*Some Inner Fury*) and Anasuya (*Possession*), Kamala Markandaya portrays the liberated women of modern India. Having been educated in England and nourished on the Western values of life, they have a regard for both the liberal and progressive ways of the West and the human ethical values of the East. They arrive at a judicious balance of the traditional and the modern ways of life to fulfil their personality. Though the conservative relations of Anasuya do not approve of her "graceless, none-too-clean, learnt-in-England ways,"[29] yet she does not feel herself cut off from the ethical values of her country like other Western-educated Indians. When Jumbo tells her about Indians who "commute between continent and continent thinking they're free, then one day they find they can't face India. London got them. Or Geneva or New York. It always does in the end," (94) she replies confidently, "But not me."

Mulk Raj Anand, who has staunch faith in Marxism and humanistic ideals, portrays heroes who though poor and downtrodden have no patience with obsolete caste prejudices and religious superstitions of their community. They have a progressive outlook on life and aspire for unshering in a new India where there are no caste differences or exploitation of the poor by the rich. Bakha the untouchable (*Untouchable*, 1935), Munoo the Coolie (*Coolie*, 1936), Lal Singh the peasant (*The Village*, 1939, *Across the Black Waters,* 1940, *The Sword and the Sickle*, 1942), and Ananta the labourer (*The Big Heart*, 1944), are all rugged individualists who suffer because they refuse to conform. Though persecuted by society for their non-conformity, they remain indomitable in their spirits. Lal Singh ridicules the ignorance and fatalism of the villagers and castigates the religious priests like Mahant Nandgir, who exploit the blind faith of the villagers for their selfish interests and benefits. Ananta, the hero of *The Big Heart* recognizes the value of machines in the modern industrial age, but also emphasizes the need for human values of fraternity and cooperation to face the evils which may creep in society because of the material progress. For him what matters is not money, but a "big heart." "There is no talk of money; one should have a big heart,"[30] he tells his fellow labourers.

In R.K.Narayan's novels, the conflict between tradition and modernity takes the form of clash between the older generation and the younger one as is evident from the difference in the outlooks of Margayya and his son Balu in *The Financial Expert* (1952), Sriram and his grandmother in *Waiting for Mahatma* (1955), Raju and his mother in *The Guide* (1958), and Jagan and his son Mali in *The Sweet Vendor* (1967). Mali who goes to America to learn the art of story-writing, outrages his father's sense of orthodox morality when he proudly describes in his letters his habit of taking beef. He even exhorts his father and other countrymen to follow his example:

> I've taken to eating beef, and I don't think I'm any the worse for it. Steak is something quite tasty and juicy. Now I want to suggest why don't you people start eating beef? It'll solve the problem of useless cattle in our country and we won't have to beg for food from America. I sometimes feel ashamed when India asks for American aid. Instead of that, why not slaughter useless cows which wander in the streets and block the traffic?[31]

He further shocks his father when he marries a half-Korean and half-American girl much against Jagan's wishes.

Moorthy in Raja Rao's *Kanthapura* (1938) embodies the blend of tradition and modernity in his character. He believes in moral values of India, but wants his countrymen to discard their outdated belief in superstitions and fatalism. He fights against untouchability and pleads for the marriage of widows. Ramaswamy, the narrator-hero of *The Serpent and the Rope* (1960), does not cease to be a South Indian Brahmin in spite of his education and stay in Britain and France for a long period. Though he marries a French girl, Madeleine, and adopts the sophisticated habits of the West, yet he remains an Indian in his outlook on life. He seeks the fulfilment of his being through the spiritualism of the East rather than the materialism of the West. Poised between the dualities of the East and the West, tradition and modernity, he, consciously or unconsciously, tries to integrate them at various levels by his beliefs and actions.

While in the novels of the Indian-English writers in general, the problem of the conflict or synthesis between tradition and modernity figures as a secondary theme, in the writings of Bhabani Bhattacharya it assumes the significance of the dominating issue in contemporary Indian life. The author analyzes the political, religious, social and economic problems of modern India through the perspective of this basic conflict in our ethos.

NOTES

1. *The Oxford English Dictionary* (Oxford: The University Press, 1961), p. 226.
2. *Funk & Wagnalls New "Standard" Dictionary of the English Language* (New York: Frank & Wagnalls, 1961), p. 2545.
3. Harry Shaw, *Concise Dictionary of Literary Terms* (New York: McGraw-Hill, 1976), p. 274.
4. S. Gopalan, *Tradition: A Social Analysis* (Madras: The University of Madras, 1973), pp. 27-28.
5. E.M. Forster, *Aspects of the Novel* (London: Edward Arnold, 1945), p. 35.
6. *Ibid.*, pp. 36-37.
7. *Ibid.*, pp. 32-33.
8. S.S. Prawer, *Comparative Literary Studies* (London: Gerald Duckworth, 1973), p. 57.
9. *Ibid.*, pp. 68-69.
10. T.S.. Eliot, "Tradition and Individual Talent," *T.S. Eliot: Three Essays,* with an introduction by Shiv K. Kumar (Calcutta: Oxford University Press, 1974), p. 16.
11. S.N. Ganguly, *Tradition, Modernity and Development* (Delhi: The Macmillan, 1977), pp. 44-45.
12. S. Gopalan, p. 9.
13. *The Oxford English Dictionary*, p. 574.
14. *Ibid.*, p. 573.
15. *Funk & Wagnalls New "Standard" Dictionary*, p. 1594.
16. Anna Balakian, "Influence and Literary Fortune," *Yearbook of Comparative and General Literature*, xi (1972), p. 29.
17. S. Gopalan, p. 4.
18. Erasmian, *The Unrest in Religion* (London: George Allen and Unwin, 1944), p. 121.
19. The tension, for example, that England experienced with industrialization acutely showed itself in literature, in Hardy and Dickens, but its nature is totally different from the tension that India experienced with the advent of modernisation.
20. S. Gopalan, p. 2.
21. *Ibid.*, pp. 2-3.
22. *Ibid.*, p. 16.
23. *The Pelican Guide to English Literature, Vol. 7 (The Modern Age)*, ed. Boris Ford (Harmondsworth, Middlesex: Penguin, 1970), p. 34.
24. Nabneeta Dev Sen, "Modernity and Tradition in Bengali Novels," *The Hindustan Times Weekly*, September 4, 1977, p. i.
25. John Press, ed. *Commonwealth Literature: Unity and Diversity in a Common Culture* (London: Heinemann, 1965), pp. 107-8.
26. S.K.Ghosh, *The Prince of Destiny* (London: Rebman, 1909), p. 597.
27. Kamala Markandaya, *A Silence of Desire* (Four Square Edition, 1966), p. 63.
28. Nayantara Sahgal, *A Time to be Happy* (Bombay: Jaico, 1963), p. 147.
29. Kamala Markandaya, *Possession* (Bombay: Jaico, 1967), p. 30.
30. Mulk Raj Anand, *The Big Heart* (Madras: C.Subbiah Chetty, 1948), p. 99.
31. R.K.Narayan, *The Sweet Vendor* (London: The Bodley Head, 1967), pp. 62-63.

The Early Novels

The fusion of the traditional and the modern values is the most conspicuous feature of Bhabani Bhattacharya's writings. Highlighting this significant characteristic in his works, K.R. Chandrasekharan aptly remarks:

> With his progressive ideas and his vision of a glorious future he has also great admiration for the spiritual and cultural heritage of the country. Like the great men whom he admired, particularly Tagore and Gandhi, he is also a builder of bridges between the present and the past.[1]

The idea of the integration of approaches and the blending of values is by far the most significant idea that Bhattacharya conveys through his novels. The study of Bhattacharya's novels from this point of view can conveniently be made in two parts: his early novels, comprising *So Many Hungers*, *Music for Mohini, He Who Rides a Tiger* and *A Goddess Named Gold,* and his later ones, viz. *Shadow from Ladakh* and *A Dream in Hawaii*. The present chapter deals with Bhattacharya's early novels. Although in his first novel, *So Many Hungers*, the novelist does not elaborate the motif of synthesis directly and primarly because of the limitations of its particular theme, yet in the remaining ones he earnestly makes a case for the blending of the traditional and the modern values of life and art.

I

In *So Many Hungers*, Bhattacharya synthesizes the old and the new values through different sets of characters and episodes. The stories of the Basu family in Calcutta and Kajoli's family in Baruni project his belief that life is all compromise, and there can, nevertheless, be unity in diversity.

The Basu family of Calcutta has six members in all. There are four males and two female members. All except one live together under the same roof. The male as well as the female members of the family are, more or less, diametrically opposed to one another with the exception of Rahoul and Devata, yet they live peacefully and happily together.

The eldest member of this family, Devesh Basu, is an earnest Gandhiite. He is an idealist and a veteran freedom fighter. Above seventy in age, he lives in a village where people are very dear to him, and he thinks them as "the core of his being, his blood and bone." (64) The villagers, too, hold him in high esteem and call him "Devata" out of love and respect. But none except Rahoul in his own family understands the old man. Rahoul's wife, Monju describes him:

> Grandfather. An eccentric. He had odd ideas. Ever since he retired from his work as a teacher at a city school he had lived by himself in a village not far from the sea; he lived like one of the peasant folk. (14)

Devata's son, Samarendra Basu, is also hostile to his father because of his involvement in national struggle for freedom. He is a materialist and hard-core realist. He is middle-aged and has a greed for money and fame like any common man. "The end justifies means," is his motto. He does not like his father's nationalistic ideas. He is a profiteer and hoarder as a businessman. Hankering after glamorous honorary titles and accumulation of riches are his greatest ambitions in life. Whereas "Devata" has wholeheartedly devoted himself to the cause of national independence, the very thought of India's freedom appears to Samarendra a hollow idea and "a crazy dream" that can never materialize. Rahoul has no sympathy with his father's dubious and unscrupulous ways to accumulate money in the critical times of World War II and the Bengal famine. He does not like Samarendra's blind faith in the British Empire and the British ways of life.

Rahoul, Samarendra's eldest son, is a scientist and an idealist, having a deep faith in the moral values of human life. Quite contrary to his father, Rahoul loves his fellow beings. He has a soft corner for the suffering masses. During the Bengal famine, he even runs a free kitchen for the destitutes, whereas his father goes on hoarding rice in order to sell it in the black market. Rahoul has a keen desire to plunge into the freedom struggle, though for the time being he keeps himself busy in his scientific researches. He is a staunch nationalist who finally throws in his lot with the struggling masses. His fiery spirit is made evident by his passionate speech to the students:

> With bitter smouldering rage he had been speaking to the students, a widening circle. . . . The anger was warm in his voice, and he had paused till his speech was cool again. "Quit" cried all India. "You have done us some good along with much evil. For the good you've done you have been paid in full. The accounts have been settled. Now, for God's sake, Quit!" (212)

Kunal, Rahoul's younger brother, is a spirited youngman. He does not bother about idealism or nationalistic fervour. He is a realist who takes life as it comes his way. But he is not a realist in Samarendra's sense of the term. Entirely different from all the members of the family, he prefers an army career. Though unperturbed by idealism, Kunal, too, has faith in certain moral values and helps a needy youngman in solving his food-problem by vacating the post he held.

Besides the male members, the female members of the Basu family, namely Rahoul's mother and his wife Monju, also have different temperaments and outlooks on life. While Rahoul's mother is a middle-aged lady of worldly wisdom, Monju is hardly above twenty-five and a novice in domestic affairs. Bhattacharya describes Rahoul's mother as a practical-minded lady. As soon as she comes to know of World War II, she is worried:

> Mother felt worry. "War? It has started then? Why? we must buy rice and mustard oil, a half-year's supply, before the grocer has an inkling. Prices will touch the sky. . . . Sugar, too. Clothing. I must get white English drill for the father and you two boys. And tinned butter, tinned fish. Strange tongue you children have. The rivers of Bengal chocked with fish – every kind, large and small – still you fancy the year-old shapes packed in tins, both you and Kunal. The strong smell!" (2)

Monju, however, lacks practical wisdom. She likes to visit hotels and restaurants, and loves to dance on a ball-room floor. She is a lady of the modern times and contrary to her mother-in-law who has an old-world view.

On analyzing the male and the women characters of Samarendra's family, one gets a clear impression that they have altogether varying temperaments, attitudes and ways and modes of life. And yet one does not see any apparent clash between them. Leaving "Devata" aside, they all lead a harmonious life. In fact, Bhattacharya succeeds remarkably in depicting them as an integrated family. There is a queer amalgam of the old and the young, the idealist and the materialist, and the imperialist and the democrat in the Basu family.

The story of Kajoli's family in Baruni also exemplifies Bhattacharya's practice of blending the traditional and the modern elements of life. Both "Devata" and Kishore are outsiders belonging to the city of Calcutta. Their ways and attitudes are different from those of the peasant family they live with. Although Devata is highly educated, enlightened and an idealist, having an entirely different family background, yet he has established such harmonious relationship with Kajoli's family that it is almost impossible to think of these people without him. He loves them very much and, in turn, they too are greatly attached to him. He does not care at all for his own kith and kin, but calls Kajoli's house as "My daughter's household." (21) Even while in prison, he feels worried about these people who were "truly his own, nearer to him than his blood kin." (99) A girl of common clay, Kajoli is not highly educated or sophisticated but there exists a great affinity between her and the old man. She and her younger brother, Onu, call him "Dadu"affectionately.

Similarly Kishore's happy union with Kajoli and their mutual adjustment with each other testify to Bhattacharya's ideas of blending the traditional and the modern values. Kishore is a modern young man, educated and enlightened. He has progressive views and has been a famous labour leader of a cotton mill at Calcutta. He has served five months's imprisonment for leading the striking workers of the mill. The peasant's work of sowing, growing and reaping paddy is alien to him. On the contrary, Kajoli is a peasant-girl of Baruni. She has never been to a school, nor is she sophisticated like a city-bred girl She is a traditional Indian girl "with a legacy of manners as old as India." (25) Kajoli's marriage with Kishore, in this way, symbolizes the fusion of the old and the new values of life.

Another instance where Bhattacharya shows the encounter of the old values with the new is the episode in which a destitute girl bares herself in order to save not only herself, but also a number of other destitutes from starvation. She is common and yet uncommon, traditional and yet modern, ideal and yet real girl of modern india. This girl appears to be unconventional and different to the reader when he finds her surrendering to the animal passions of the alien soldiers. But she becomes one of the extraordinary ones when she spends all her hard-earned money to feed the starving destitutes – her fellow brethern in misery. While demeaning herself on physical level, she exalts herself on the human level. The destitutes in the alley acknowledge her angelic sacrifice and see the Mother-image in her. She, however, sheds her extraordinariness when she sits down among the destitutes and eats her own share of bread.

The episode where Rahoul addresses the peasant woman (Kajoli's mother) as "Mother" is also symbolic of the synthesis of the traditional and the modern values in the sense that Rahoul, a sophisticated man of the town, mixes up with a woman of common clay, and also that as an educated and city-bred man, he establishes his kinship with the simple and uneducated village woman. Bhattacharya expresses this idea through the dialogue between them:

> "Father is well? Mother?" She asked out of politeness "Bau-ma (daughter-in-law)? The little one?" "Yes Mother, they are well." Mother! The word had slipped his tongue without thought. Happiness came upon him that he had broken out of his class sophistication and called a simple peasant woman mother. What was there in this woman of a Bengal village, not unlike others of her kind, that he had the urge to call her mother?
>
> The peasant mother had tears in her eyes because of his kindness. (99-100)

Thus Bhattacharya presents a blending of tradition and modernity subtly but impressively in *So Many Hungers*.

II

Bhattacharya's second novel, *Music for Mohini,* is a detailed study in the old and the new values of life in Indian society. The novel deals with Indian society which is in the melting-pot because of various conflicting ideologies, each being championed by one group or another. Here, Bhattacharya puts forward the view that a reconciliation between the contrary ideals and values – modern and traditional – can lead to a happy and harmonious life. In order to bring out the virtues of moderation and integration, and to emphasize his major theme of blending the modern and the conventional, the novelist uses the dialectical method of contrast in depicting his characters.

There are two sets of characters: first, those who uphold the old, established values of the past and secondly, those who plead for a change and deviation from the dead past in favour of the new and unconventional value-pattern that suits the modern age. The novelist juxtaposes different antagonistic characters in order to bring out their ideological conflict, and then finally leads them towards a reconciliation so as to create a harmony in life.

In the earlier part of the novel, as the story unfolds itself at Mohini's parental home, her father, the Professor, is shown in conflict with Old Mother. Mohini's father is a highly educated and modern-minded man. He is inspired by the norms and fashions of the modern times. He gets his daughter, Mohini, admitted to a Christian convent school, and also allows her to become a radio singer. He does not see any harm in Mohini's songs being recorded and sold in open market. But his mother – Old Mother – is very much opposed to this wide publicity of his granddaughter. She is above seventy, conservative and rigid in outlook. She has a blind faith in orthodoxy and superstitions, and is a staunch supporter of the old and established moral values. The old lady does not like her son's ideas which appear odd to her. When he does not pay heed to her, she threatens to renounce the world. The situation threatens to turn inflammable, but the Professor handles it tactfully. Though there is a truce for the time being, but the real crisis occurs on the question of Mohini's marriage. As the Professor is a man of modern ideas, he naturally wants to marry his daughter to an educated, urban-bred and cultured boy. He rejects outright two proposals because the former party demanded a heavy dowry and the latter one comprises the uncultured lot who examine Mohini physically as if she were an article for sale in an auction. Then there arrives a third party. This time the prospective groom comes with his friends. All of them are bright youngmen, good-mannered, gracious and courteous. Having seen the girl, they approve her. The Professor appreciates the boy wholeheartedly, and agrees to marry Mohini to him. But Old Mother does not lke the match at all. There ensues a conflict in the family. Bhattacharya describes the discord as follows:

> His voice was joyous and proud. "Mother, we've found the right match for our girl. Look up the almanac for an auspicious day."
>
> Old mother was silent for a time, her face withdrawn and grave.
>
> "Why, surely, you approve — "
>
> "No, childling," She shook her head with quite decision. "He is not the right sort for our Mohini. He and his friends have no respect for elders. They smoked cigarettes in your presence, didn't they?
>
> . . . No, our girl has not been trained up in their un-Indian way, even if she has read at a Christian convent school. She will be a misfit in that fast circle.
>
> "But, Mother, the groom — "
>
> "The groom belongs to his circle. He has his roots in that soil. They are all alike. No tradition, no ture culture. Apes of Westernism!"
>
> His patience gave way. His face darkened. "Let our girls remain unwed," he cried harshly, "rather than be sacrificed to your antiquated outlook."
>
> Old Mother's face was a picture of rage. Her eyelids flickered and her gentle mouth stiffened.
>
> "Send me away to the Holy City. I won't have no mouthful of your food, or let water pass my lips." (44)

As a consequence of this difference in outlook the issue of marriage is left unsettled, and Mohini remains unwed. The difference between the mother and the son are, however, soon after resolved when Jayadev appears on the scene and is found to be the most suitable groom for Mohini. He is accepted not only by the Professor and Old Mother, but also by Mohini herself as he combines in him the traditional as well as the modern values in being both "a great scholar and master of Behula village." (50)

The Professor also synthesizes the old and the modern values in his character. That is why he often yields to Old Mother's outdated notions and somewhat silly actions. Out of his traditional love for his mother, he cannot "bear the thought of Old Mother going away" and thinks: "Better let her have her own way in the house." (16) He knows full well that the path of compromise is the better one, and that one cannot always do without the old values of life. In order to live happily with the old lady he even lets her tie an amulet to his neck-chain. When with the old lady's help, Mohini's marriage is settled with Jayadev, the Professor gratefully acknolwedges:

> "The old customs and conventions are not too unsound," he said. For once the son, out of his heart's fullness, graciously conceded to his mother's wisdom. "They seem to suit our mental climate." (55-56)

Similarly, Old Mother is also well aware of the limits of her power. She, too, does not rigidly adhere to her outdated and conservative ideas always. As soon as she sees the tension mounting in the family, she realizes the danger and immediately relents in her attitude to accommodate the new beliefs and practices. In most of the matters, however, she tries to have her own way. Despite all her sour defeats over Mohini, Old Mother feels content when her son agrees to have a charm tied to her neck-chain:

> Old Mother took one good look at the slim gold chain on his neck with its pendant amulet. He mocked many of the old beliefs, but the amulet was there to shield him from the Evil Eye. He had firmly refused to wear it until she had wielded that weapon of hers, "Send me away to the Holy City." It was, indeed, one of her major triumphs. (18)

Even the Old Mother is not very rigid in her attitude towards modern values. The novelist observes that "Old Mother had compromised with modernity" and was "of the old and of the new." (130) This old lady upholds old values and orthodox ways only as a habit, otherwise she is often ready to compromise with the spirit of the new times. Bringing this fact to light, Bhattacharya remarks:

> Every Sunday evening the family went to the cinema, often an Indian film, though Old Mother, with all her orthodox heart, enjoyed English pictures as well – the "shadow-show' was to her

> mind a wonder of wonders, the supreme achievement of the Western people. (30)

Thus the novelist synthesizes the old values with the new ones in the persons of the Professor and the Old Mother, showing that "on many points of orthodox living they had reached a fair adjustment." (16)

Mohini is happily married to Jayadev and comes to Behula as the new mistress of the Big House. Here she again ecounters the old values personified in her mother-in-law. Mohini is a girl of the modern times. She is city-bred, suave, convent-educated and an upcoming radio-star whose songs have been recorded and displayed in public. She is a beautiful girl who likes all the good things of life. She judges the world around her in terms of aesthetic values. Her heart is full of love for her husband, and she wants to be admired and loved by him in turn.

Jayadev, who is a visionary and an idealist, expects his wife to be different from an ordinary young woman with basic physical needs and requirements. He sees her as "Gargi" or "Maitreyi," "no household drudge, nor decorative being, but an intellectual, striding besides man in a tireless quest for knowledge." (71) Though frustrated in her ambition to lead glamorous life, Mohini does not give vent to her dissatisfaction. She is resilient by nature and soon overcomes her dejection. Though aware of her limitation, she endeavours to rise to the expectation of her husband, and even starts taking lessons from him in Sanskrit. Though she is fatigued with these "tiresome" lessons, and has to abandon them, she is not disheartened. She knows that her married life can be peaceful and meaningful only if she adjusts herself to the wishes of her husband, shares his ideals and renders him positive help in his programme of social re-construction. Thus Mohini not only comes closer to Jayadev, but also rescues the backward, ignorant and illiterate rural women from the darkness of orthodox living, and shows them a glimpse of the modern times.

Mohini also works for bringing about a fusion of the old and the new values in the lives of the womenfolk of Behula. The village women identify the young mistress of the Big House with themselves. They exclaim:

> Their own, their joy, their joy and pride, and she was so human, without any of the plumage of the rich, whose distant look bespoke that they tried the blue pathways of the sky! (150)

By identifying herself with the women of the village, she brings the Big House closer to the ordinary houses of Behula. Mohini thus tries to prove worthy of her husband and establishes deep communion with him. Bhattacharya describes this communion by making Jayadev sit on the very tree-perch on which Mohini used to sit daily. It is a symbolic act, suggesting a union of beings.

Besides Jayadev, Mohini has to adjust herself to the obsolete ideas and superstitious beliefs of her stubborn mother-in-law too Known as "Mother" in the village, this old lady is in a way the ruthless past reincarnated. She is all for the family tradition. In reality Mother represents the Big House which is "much more than a residence . . . a way of living, a stern discipline and iron tradition." (78) Jayadev has already made Mohini aware of the fact that she will have to adjust herself to a great extent to the traditional life-pattern of the Big House:

> "The Big House will make heavy demands on its young mistress," he warned her tenderly. "Demands that you'II find unreasonable. Some of them will have to be met with patience and a spirit of give-and-take." (78)

At first Mohini finds life at the Big House almost unbearable. As she has been brought up in an altogether different type of environment, she has to struggle hard "to retouch her mental values, readjust her expectations" (108) before she is able to accommodate herself comfortably at Behula. She is ridiculed by the women of Behula for her clothes. Her mother-in-law is stern and exacting and puts a number of restraints upon the young girl. Mohini's wearing of a gay-coloured sari, as it becomes a new bride, irritates her. She likes to see Mohini all covered by a white cotton sheet instead of a mill-made sari. The Mother tells her that modern songs make no sense and that she should sing only religious songs. Again she objects to her son's bride climbing a tree-perch as it is a very unbecoming thing for the young mistress of the Big House. She does not like Mohini wearing the glass and lac bangles instead of those made of pure gold. Thus "there was no end to prohibitions" (130) and restraints on Mohini. Subdued by these prohibitions, Mohini strives hard to adjust to the old ways and modes of life in the rural society and in this process she, too, changes unawares. Bhattacharya affirms:

> Yes, the young mistress of the Big House took deeper colour from her new life everyday. Slowly she fitted herself to the rural design. Her sprightliness, her quick girlish laugh, she easily subdued. The mother was a ruthless teacher. (130)

Owing to her mother-in-law's sternness and old-world spirit, Mohini sometimes feels sore about her behaviour, but with the passage of time she begins to realize that the Mother is not completely devoid of the basic qualities: compassion and sacrifice. She, therefore, overcomes initial hurdles and develops a great love and sympathy for the old lady:

> Yet, Mohini told herself, perhaps she judged the mother too harshly? Perhaps she saw the wrong side of this old tapestry of tradition and missed the design? Duty and compassion were not at odds in the mother; the key to the design was sacrifice which was a right and privilege, not a duty alone. (173)

Gradually, the struggle between the contrasting values that is so intense and fierce in the beginning becomes less and less severe, and resolves finally into a happy compromise. Both Mohini and her mother-in-law, representing the modern and the traditional values respectively, begin to understand each other better and live amicably.

The Mother also realizes that it is the age of the young men and women with their new ideals and aspirations, and hence she, too, changes. She starts moulding her ideas so as to cope with the requirements of the new age. She is reconciled to her son and Mohini as soon as she comes to know from Harindra of Mohini's pregnancy. Both the old and the young mistresses of the Big House thus reach at the perfect harmony with each other. Commenting on their adjustment, Bhattacharya remarks:

> Meantime, in the Big House, a sweet intimacy built on their common dream linked Mohini with the mother. It was as though they were two conspirators filled with one secret. Everything else, the movements and gestures of workaday life, was a covering shell. (144)

It is not that Bhattacharya always makes his younger characters submit before the aged ones in his bid to present the mutual adjustment. He makes his old characters also realize in their turn genuine demands of the new age. Jayadev's mother, too, begins to feel that her son is right and justified in his ideas and actions, and that the values to which she rigidly adheres count no more in the modern times. The only possible way to end all discord in life seems to her in a compromise between her old beliefs and the new values of life upheld by her son and daughter-in-law. She and Jayadev have previously been in constant conflict with each other because of their contrasting ideas and outlooks. She has been an ardent supporter and defender of the family traditions, whereas Jayadev has a liberal outlook. He knows that the conflict between him and his mother is an inevitable and difficult one as it is not a clash of personalities, but that of values, of tradition and modernity. Subsequently, this conflict turns serious when the mother attempts to make Mohini offer her heart's blood to the Virgin Goddess. Jayadev, who comes to know of the incident in time, snubs the mother and tells her that they are not slaves of the stars, that there is "no room in the Big House for crazy beliefs" (179) and that the whole village looks towards the people of the Big House for a proper way of living. The infuriated mother, too, in her turn, scolds him that he is degenerate and she is ashamed to have him as her son. She further says: "I know your mind. Heresy holds you. Old beliefs, old morals, old values mean nothing to you." (180) Jayadev makes it clear to her that there are "values beyond your grasp, since you'll always try to reach them with your reason, never with your feelings. Life has punished you. . . . Blind belief shapes your thinking; blind belief cannot make a sentiment." (180) Thus there is a fierce ideological tussle between the mother and the son. But soon the mother realizes that her son's path is the right one:

> for the first time, she could see her son clearly. His ideas, his point of view, moulded by the new spirit in the land, were different from hers and opposed to them, but they were, nonetheless, true ideals. (187)

This realization or the "moment of insight" brings the mother nearer to Jayadev, and there prevails an atmosphere of cordiality and mutual understanding in the Big House. The discord between the mother and the son, the mother-in-law and the daughter-in-law, and the husband and the wife ends. Bhattacharya concludes:

> At last, there was no discord. Life was music – a note of song for the Old Mother was in her, a note for Jayadev and his rebel gods, a note for the Big House and Behula village, torn and at cross-purpose for a while. Her life was music – the quest for every woman, her deepest need. (188)

The synthesis of the old and the new values is also evident in the story of Harindra's family. Harindra's father, the old *Kaviraj*, has been practising the ancient Indian *Ayurvedic* system of medicine for over forty years. He considers this medical system very efficacious as a cure for all sorts of diseases. But his son, Harindra, is a full-fledged surgeon, educated and trained in a Western-style medical college. Often he argues with his father that his rigid ideas about the supremacy of the Ayurvedic medical system over all the others are false and funny. He pleads with the old man that modern medicines are more efficacious in curing diseases. But his father is furious with rage because "here was a challenge to the indigenous system of *Ayurveda,* the system that had prevailed for the millenium,... To think that his son should be a carrier of the alien contamination:... What madness had come upon him that he had sent his son to town and let him study at a medical school where they cut up live rats and dissected corpses." (140) The old man openly ridicules his son and his ideas. However, later he recognizes the efficacy of the modern Allopathic medical system when he fails to cure his ailing wife. The old man has been trying Ayurvedic medicines on the patient for quite a few days, never allowing his son to treat her with the western medicines. But when her condition deteriorates more and more, and all hopes of her survival are lost, he yields to Harindra's wishes to treat her. The miracle happens and the mother's life is saved. The old man lives happily with his wife and son, quite reconciled to the modern values and systems.

The crocodile episode also exposes the hollowness of superstitions and old beliefs of people. The pool of Shiva's Temple in Behula is covered with green hyacinth and has become utterly useless for the village people. Harindra and other comrades want to remove the evil growth from the pond, but the priest of the temple sternly opposes it. He is a man of orthodox nature, and his mind is laden with conservative ideas. He has concocted a story that an accursed devotee of Shiva resides in the pond in the form of a crocodile, and it will be a sin to tease and oppress the holy spirit by removing the hyacinth from the pond. Accidentally, the little son of his daughter is lost one day and the grief-stricken mother feels deeply concerned about him. She apprehends that the crocodile of the pond has devoured the boy. The villagers accompanied by Harindra reach the pond and start removing its hyacinth. This time the priest does not object at all. All the weedy growth is removed by the morning and the pond's water shines clear. But the boy or the crocodile are not found. After a short while the boy approaches the scene. He is riding a donkey and is accompanied by a farmer of the nearby village. The daughter of the priest is besides herself with joy and does not mind when she learns that her son has committed sacrilege by eating forbidden food, fish:

> "I ate fish," the boy cried in a sort of triumph to his mother as she held him clasped in her arms. She gazed misty-eyed at him and the tears of joy ran down her cheeks. Fish was forbidden food. (160)

Jayadev, the chief protagonist in the novel, believes in the integration of the traditional and the modern values. He is both a "great scholar and master of Behula village." (50) As a "scholar" he is sensitive to modern liberal and progressive ideas, while as the "master' of the Big House he symbolizes the old traditions in his personality. Though rooted in the past, he does not lose sight of his vision of the new dawn:

> In some ways he was one with his ancestors, those strange men in ageing oil paint. Yet he was unbowed, unfettered by his inheritance. (148)

Jayadev embodies in his character the best of the Indian and the Western values. He is deeply devoted to the task of creating a harmony between the Oriental and the Occidental value-pattern. "It was his dream to reorientate the values and patterns of Hindu life." (67)

Jayadev is well-versed in the old Indian culture, but his desire is to extract the essence of our tradition, and blend it with the spirit of our own times. He has a keen desire to build up a new society based on the integration of the best elements of all thoughts and beliefs in India:

> Jayadev would break the crust of the vulgarity and reveal ancient thought in its true splendour. But the new man of his vision, growing to his full stature, was not to be a hollow reincarnation,

> not a spiritless copy of ancient Hindu man. That were as stupid as Hindu moulded in a Western pattern. (68)

He dreams about a fusion of the past with the present. It is his earnest wish to create "a profound union of today with yesterday." (78) Jayadev does not altogether negate the importance of the past in the modern times, but thinks that it is only because of yesterday that today exists. He wants to reshape the Indian society, but also recognizes the significant role of the ancient lore in the whole process of social reconstruction. He emphasizes:

> Look back that you may look forward. Look to the roots of India in this fateful hour of flowering. Use the buried material of the past to write the new social charter. (68)

Jayadev's is thus the message of synthesis between the old and the new values. The Professor, too, sees him as the product of this synthesis and tells Mohini: "He has true legacy of the past, in inner health, a source of graceful living, and to that he has added our modern culture." (130) There is an autobiographical touch about Jayadev's character.[2] The author and his persona are identical in their attitude to life.

Being village-bred and city-wed, Rooplekha also combines in her character the traditional and the modern values. When Mohini doubts the plausibility of the fusion of the city and the village, representing the modern and the traditional value-patterns respectively, Rooplekha emphatically remarks that such a union is worthwhile:

> Rooplekha held Mohini in the warmth of her smile. "Shall I answer you? We who're so wed, serve some real purpose. It is as though we made a bridge between two banks of the river. We connect culture with culture Mohini, our old Eastern view of life with the new semi-Western outlook. The city absorbs a little of the 'barbaric' village, the village absorbs a little of the 'West-polluted' city. Both change, unaware. They are less angry with each other. This is more urgent today than ever before. Our new India must rest on this foundation." (93-94)

Thus Bhabani Bhattacharya quite successfully blends the two contrary values – tradition and modernity – in *Music for Mohini*, and the novel virtually becomes the novelist's plea to such a fusion in every sphere of life.

III

He Who Rides a Tiger also presents the blending of the traditional and the modern values. Casteism or castelessness? Faith or no faith? The pendulum remains swinging from one extreme to the other throughout the story, and is finally set at rest with a synthesis of all the contrarieties.

Through the story of Kalo, the hero of the novel, Bhabani Bhattacharya illustrates that neither a rigid adherence to the established social code nor an abrupt break from it is beneficial to man. The true happiness and fulfilment in life can be attained only after a moderation of temperament – with a due regard for the established conventions and an equal awareness of the requirements of the modern age.

Kalo, the blacksmith of Jharna town, is a simple man. He has a firm faith in the traditional values of life. The caste hierarchy is sunk deep in his spirit and his "roots were deep in the age-richened soil of his own caste." (16) Though unable to understand the validity or the utility of the established social order, Kalo has never questioned its existence. His is a simple set of values. Honesty, hard-work and faith in law and justice are the core of his being. He is "a man of accepted convention" having roots "deep into age-old habits of mind and belief." (43) But after sometime, an unhappy turn of events and odd circumstances shake his faith in the existing social set-up. He wants to know why there is so much injustice and inhumanity in society. And when he is at loss to find an answer, the very "questions spread like some corroding acid over the faith, the values by which he had lived." (53) The oppressive awareness of his low birth, poverty, hunger, three months's rigorous imprisonment for a petty offence, his work as a brothel-house agent, and last but not the least, Lekha's degradation and humiliation in the harlot-house, are the factors which turn Kalo into a social rebel.

Disillusioned about the sense of social justice, Kalo metamorphoses himself. He casts away the old values by which he has lived his past life and wages war against the entire social system:

> His battle was with the accuser, the centuries-old tradition, from which had come the inner climate of his being. . . . Kalo had not only to deny but to eradicate the values by which he had been bred. He had to cut his social taproot and give up his inheritance. (71)

He renounces his caste and becomes a twice-born by wearing the nine-stranded sacred Brahminic thread across his chest. In this way, the slow-witted and conservative "Kamar" revolts against "tradition." He feels himself free from his spiritual bondage:

> With that gesture he had thrown off the heavy yoke of his past and flouted the three thousand years of his yesterdays. Putting on the sacred thread he had made himself rootless. The terror of that act was followed by a deep sense of release. He had transcended the station that birth and blood had assigned him. Exhilaration and new courage filled him. (81)

With his "release" from the oppressive bondage of class and caste, Kalo emerges a modern man. No more does he think a Brahmin superior and God's chosen one. He starts believing in the modern man's faith in equality between man and man, and tells Viswanath: "All men are born equal." (110)

But this situation does not continue for long, and soon afterwards, the past starts haunting him. Though Kalo in the Brahminic garb moves on a new plane in society, the "Kamar" within him remains alive and intact. There erupts a battle between his two contradictory faces: Mangal Adhikari and Kalo, representing the new and the old ways of life respectively. Sometimes Kalo feels that "a true god was in the sanctum. The trick by which he had installed a fake was unreal, false, better forgotten. Kalo as Mangal Adhikari had truly attained reincarnation." (100) But at other times, he also identifies himself with Viswanath, and thus has "nothing but irreverence for the temple and all it stood for." (115)

This inner conflict continues in Kalo's mind until it becomes unbearable to him. The moment comes when Kalo has to make a manly decision "to kill the tiger" (226) and thereby descend to solid earth from his lofty seat. His daughter, Chandra Lekha, bent upon destroying herself for his sake, further forces his decision, and finally, he reveals the astounding truth: "I who made this temple was not born a Brahmin." (225) The crisis of his spirit ends and Kalo becomes his real self again.

Although "out of the nine-petalled stone lotus" Kalo walks "down to the soft earth," (232) and thus returns from where he had started his journey, he is no more the Kalo of the past now. There is a big change in him. His outlook has been broadened. He is disillusioned and awakened. No more does he feel inferior to any one in caste or social status:

> Never again would the smith be despised, mocked, trampled upon. Never again. For the fetters of his mind had been cut. The look in his eyes was clear and undazzled. (226)

Thus Kalo comes to synthesize the old and the new in his personality.

The blending between the traditional and the modern values is also evident at the end of the novel when B-10 and Viswanath return and stand united with Kalo in his hour of decision. Both of them are two facets of Kalo's self, the former representing the unconventional and the latter symbolizing the conventional elements in Kalo. He has his leanings to and attachment for both of them. B-10 is an ideal man and a hero for him. Though he has not known B-10 for long, yet he says: "I have faith in him." (141) He finds himself identical with B-10 in the sense that both are craftsmen, working with their hands. Besides B-10, Kalo has in him something of Viswanath also. Bhattacharya expresses that "a curious fellow-feeling rose sometimes in him (Kalo) and cut the distance between them." (115) It is the spontaneous fellow-feeling between two persons of the same caste and profession out of which Kalo, despite his Brahminic posture, has "identified himself with Viswanath." (115)

As soon as both Viswanath and B-10 leave him, Kalo is faced with an utter emotional crisis. The moment of their rejoining him is the moment of Kalo's emerging victorious out of this spiritual crisis. Thus there is a blending of the unconventional and the conventional elements in Kalo's person.

The union of Chandra Lekha with B-10 is another instance of the blending between the traditional and the modern elements of life in the sense that it will be a union of the lowest and the highest. While the possibilities of this marriage are being explored, Kalo underlines

Bhattacharya's own philosophy of synthesis when he observes: "In life, sometimes, a big compromise has to be made." (182)

IV

In his next novel, *A Goddess Named Gold*, Bhabani Bhattacharya deals with the theme of economic freedom of hungry masses and warns against the evils of profiteering and poverty which, if not completely eradicated, may defeat the very purpose of freedom and lead to many more hungers. With the freedom in sight, people have to work with solidarity and faith to ameliorate their lot and make their country prosperous. They have also to be on their guard against the greedy rich men who may exploit freedom for their own selfish ends. Atmaram, the holy minstrel, remarks with foresight: "Freedom is the beginning of the road where there was no road. But the new road swarms with robbers." (119)

The theme of the confrontation of the old and the new values acquires a new dimension in this novel for it shows the resurgence of the village women. Though Lakshmi is the wife of a Seth, yet at heart she is with the village women. She has gone to prison with them in the Quit India days and identifies herself with their aspirations. Sohagi proclaims:

> You are the Seth's wife Lakshmi, but you are also our sister.(256)

She represents the modern resurgent women who fight for their rights and against social injustice. She leads the village women in their march against her husband – the Seth who does not sell cloth at a fair price. She believes in the idea of equal rights for men and women and, as such, takes active part in Meera's plan to win the cinema show, denied by the Seth, for the village women. Whenever Lakshmi supports the cause of the poor and pleads vehemently with her husband for sympathy towards them, the Seth yields before her much against his will. She is against her husband because of his greed, money-making and unsympathetic attitude towards the poor. She is otherwise a traditional Indian woman who is very much devoted to her husband.

Atmaram, another important character in the novel, combines spiritual faith and modern outlook on life in his character. He is "one like many others in Sonamitti, yet far apart. Owning nothing, he had the dignity of a king." (61) The minstrel is of the past and of the present simultaneously. He is a song-maker who sings to folks and thus keeps the ancient folklore alive to them. Hence there is a continuity of the past in his character. The minstrel is also aware of the existing social conditions and the malpractices of the rich people who exploit the common masses for their own vested interests. Unequal distribution of land among people makes him brood:

> This fruit-giving earth. Enough earth for all if shared fairly. So much belongs to so few. The same tale everywhere. One man owns half a village; the tillers have the rest in five hundred morsels. (69)

Knowing the significance of the terms "vote" and "election" full well, he warns Meera lest Sonamitti people elect the Seth as their representative to the District Board. He is "a homeless, ever-wandering minstrel" (115) who does not live only for himself or his kith and kin, but thinks about the welfare of the whole mankind. He stays away from his home for long stretches of time, dwelling in the dreamland of mystic nature. He is, however, not altogether cut off from his people. Often he feels that he has "more to get from the village than from all the world." (65) This feeling forces him to return off and on to Sonamitti where he guides the people in their daily affairs with his practical wisdom.

The minstrel is a Gandhian idealist who wants better life-conditions for the masses in the country. He has an ardent wish "to wipe every tear from every eye." (75) He is, however, a practical-minded person, and is fully aware of the danger to his people from the Seth's unscrupulous ways. The invention of the touchstone fable and the act of giving the amulet to Meera show the minstrel's practical wisdom. Through it, he is able to save not only his own family, but the entire village from the Seth's deadly clutches. The minstrel goes on "following a middle course" (72) between two ways of life, and exemplifies a happy synthesis of the old and the new elements in his character.

Meera also combines the old values and the modern outlook in her character. Bhattacharya has drawn in her "a girl from storybooks, both real and unreal." (110) With the gold that she fancies to get after the touchstone has worked, she plans to help all the people of Sonamitti. When Sohan Lal comes to know that she wants to be kind to all the people who need help, he warns her against her impractical views. But

Meera has a core of realism in her. She has not always been a visionary. It is her teen-age that has made her dwell in the dreamland. "Her belief (in touchstone) came plainly from a wish every young girl has, that some wonder happen to her and her life be changed." (175) She is a politically-conscious girl and has even gone to prison in the Quit India Movement at the age of ten. Bold in spirit, she rescues Nago from the well. She is against the Seth who exploits the poor people, and launches a successful campaign forcing him to sell cloth at fair price. She knows that the times are changing and no woman can afford to be timid now. She is a votary of the equality of rights for male and female, and as such, foils the Seth's plan to keep women away from the cinema-show. She tells the Seth in his face:

> "We outwitted you." She hesitated a little. "We had to do it. Equal rights for men and women, that was the song. We had to fight for that song." (148)

Meera rids herself of her fancy as soon as she becomes aware of its ill consequences. She discards the amulet and throws it into the river.

Meera's prospective marriage with Sohan Lal symbolizes the union of a rural girl with an urban youth. While Sohan Lal has served in the army during the World War and seen enough of life, Meera has remained confined to village. While Meera has deep faith in the touchstone and its power to turn copper into gold, Sohan Lal is unimpressed by it. He often pleads with Meera to see reason, but she because of her genuine interest to help people by the gold acquired through amulet remains adamant:

> Listen, Meera. With your gold you will save this village. You will save the seven villages. But there are eight hundred thousand others. Each has a Seth of its own. Each Seth waits to snatch the new power from the people. You cannot have gold enough to save India. (197)

Whereas Sohan Lal is an educated and enlightened youth of the city, Meera is an almost uneducated girl of the village. In fact, their coming close to each other and finally deciding to marry signifies the blending of the two contrarieties: city and village, representing the modern and the traditional ways of life respectively. Highlighting the polarities in life and emphasizing the need for their synthesis, Bhabani Bhattacharya remarks:

> Good and evil were dwelling side by side, one a foil for the other. Light needed darkness. Ugliness enhanced beauty. Riches were so welcome because of the all-pervasive poverty. What use was a healer in the absence of ailment? Where was the pleasure in giving, if no one would beg and receive? (280)

NOTES

1. Chandrasekharan, p. 8.
2. Lila Ray, p. 74. She observes: "Jayadev was a solitary man, silent, with dreamy, heavy-lidded eyes set in a young tranquil face. He is essentially a scholar. His clean-cut mouth and chin reflect the firmness of his purpose. He is gentle, a little shy, endearingly absentminded. This description fits his creator, Bhabani Bhattacharya very aptly. Jayadev is the only one of his characters which bears an autobiographical resemblance to him."

The Later Novels

Bhattacharya's later novels, *Shadow from Ladakh* and *A Dream in Hawaii,* also deal with the conflict between the traditional and the modern values. In a way, the major linking factor of his later fiction with its earlier counterpart is the treatment of the tradition-modernity theme. Though widely different from the preceding novels in the subject-matter, technique, style and language, Bhattacharya's later creative endeavours form an inseparable part of the mainstream through the treatment of this theme.

I

The synthesis of the Indian spiritual values and the Western modernism, is undoubtedly the central theme of Bhattacharya's celebrated novel, *Shadow from Ladakh.* This novel "preaches by implication . . . that India needs a blending of divergent sets of values if she is to cope with the challenge of the times."[1] More explicitly, there has to be in Indian life a synthesis of tradition and modernity – asceticism and worldliness, village and city, and the East and the West, in order to ensure the country's progress and security.

As the plot of the novel unfolds itself, the clash between the traditional and the modern values becomes evident in the form of the discord between Gandhigram and Steeltown. Steeltown, gaining in importance because of the Chinese aggression, starts expanding rapidly, and its surveyors and draftsmen measure and draw maps of the pasture-land adjoining the village, Gandhigram. The village people are annoyed at it. They plan to oppose any such move because they think that the people from Steeltown are unable to comprehend what the village stands for. For them, it is simply a tract of land that can easily be acquired. The people of Gandhigram, however, think the village to be a symbol having deep meaning:

> The apparently insignificant village was building up a model for the whole of India. The new community of people was creating a

> social order in which all were truly equal. All land belonging to the cooperative. Food from the fields distributed according to needs. Other needs met by small industries based locally, economic self-sufficiency was the set aim.[2]

These people are averse to big industries. They have deep faith in Gandhian economics. Satyajit Sen, the guiding spirit of Gandhigram, meets Bhashkar Roy, the Chief Engineer of Steeltown, and expresses his concern over the unhappy developments. Bhashkar, an America-trained engineer, disagrees with him and tells him that in order to attain economic self-sufficiency and safeguard India's freedom, the establishment of big industries as well as large-scale steel production are essential. He argues:

> Steel means economic progress. Machine tools, tractors, big industrial plants, locomotives. Steel to fight poverty and hunger. But steel has gained a second meaning. It stands for our country's freedom. That is an inescapable fact, not to be changed by wishful thinking. Development plus defence – a compulsion of our current history.

Bhashkar thinks Gandhigram "a road-block in the path of progress," (200) and for him "the assault on Gandhigram was ideologic, not economic." (200) He is of the view that Gandhigram has no relevance in modern times. It is his earnest wish to let life be "easier, freer, and happier" (60) instead of being choked with taboos. He is convinced that after enjoying the modern facilities which are available to the city people, the village folk will certainly favour Steeltown type of life. They will start adopting new ways of life, and thus gradually Gandhigram will be merged into the pattern of Steeltown. In fact, with this act Bhashkar captures Satyajit's own weapon – the weapon of non-violence. Satyajit and the people of Gandhigram are baffled at his move. However, being a true Gandhiite, Satyajit cannot and does not stop people from going to see the cultural programme at the Meadow House, for it amounts to violence in his opinion.

The inmates of Gandhigram enjoy the programmes and finally conclude that there should be a cultural communion between them and the people of Steeltown, that the old and the new values must freely intermingle so as to make life meaningful, and that no single culture should dominate other cultures as envisaged by Gandhi:

> I refuse to be blown off my feet, though I do not propose merely to feed on the ancient cultures of our land; we have to enrich our old traditions with the experience of the new times. But the alien elements in their turn will have to be affected by the spirit of the soil. One dominant culture absorbing the rest – that cannot make for harmony; that will be an artificiality and forced unity. That we do not want. (156)

As Satyajit is a devoted follower of Mahatma Gandhi, he too believes in a healthy synthesis of the old traditions and the new elements in life. He duly recognizes the vital role of Steeltown in the national prosperity. In his opinion Gandhigram will take the lead when Steeltown has finished its race. He asserts:

> Steeltown belongs to the present, Gandhigram to the future. Steeltown must do its work. But when that work is done, when the material benefits of production have been fully attained, Steeltown, decrepit and soulless, will have to seek new moorings. Then it will be Gandhigram's turn to come forward. (156)

In this sense, both Steeltown and Gandhigram are complementary to each other and not completely opposed. If the former is "body," the latter is its "spirit." One cannot do without the other. The contention that "Body and spirit must be fed together, not turn by turn" (157) implies that there must be a blending of the new and the old values, represented by Steeltown and Gandhigram respectively.

Suruchi also pleads for a synthesis of traditional and modern values of life. Bhattacharya writes: "she had not accepted Gandhigram in its entirety. But she had not rejected it, either." (273) She believes in the Tagorian philosophy of the fusion of diverse elements of life, and recalls:

> Integration – that was the poet's life-long quest: integration of the simple and the sophisticated; the ancient and the modern; city and village; East and West. (215)

Suruchi, however, does not appreciate Gandhigram's rigid adherence to the outdated morals and conventions. According to her, there must be a synthesis of the old and the new in the life of the village. She reflects:

> There was one way left for Gandhigram. It must make readjustments. That would mean acceptance of life in its totality. But not the Steeltown way: that also was denial of life deep under the surface. Let license be chastened by restraint. Let restraint find its right level by a leavening of freedom. Let there be a meeting ground of the two extremes: Let each shed some of its content and yet remain true to itself. (274)

Satyajit, too, has definite views about the integration of values. His desire is, however, to bring about a healthy synthesis of the two modes of life. When he sees Dalai Lama at Darjeeling, Satyajit makes it clear to him:

> What has alienated us from Tibetan way of life is the semifeudal pattern of society. A relic of the old world cannot lie within the shell of the new; under the hard pressure it's bound to be crushed into pulp. (295)

Even Satyajit's daughter, Sumita, is not against electricity, the power to turn the wheel of modern industrial revolution. Realizing its importance to the modern civilization, she herself begins to learn about electricity. Bhashkar is astonished to note:

> The ease with which she could resolve all contradictions in her mind. Machines were the enemy. Yet she was fascinated by the very life spark in machines – electricity. The life spark, the energy that had begotten the new century, the new civilization. (142)

With the passage of time, understanding dawns upon Bhashkar. The contact with Sumita and the Chinese girls makes him comprehend the values that Satyajit symbolizes:

> A new insight had come – he had begun to understand Satyajit. Some of the things he stood for. (284)

Bireswar Basu, Satyajit's close friend, calls Bhashkar a *phenomenon*, and tells Satyajit that both of them are complementary to each other like light and darkness in the hour of twilight. They may be opposite to one another, but one alone is useless without the other.

The novelist resolves the conflicts between Steeltown and Gandhigram towards the end of the novel. As the news about Satyajit's fast unto death reaches Steeltown, the millhands are at once full of indignation against Steeltown. Bhashkar senses the danger and withdraws the plan of encroaching upon the land of Gandhigram. He even reckons it as the fulfilment of his long-cherished dream of bringing Steeltown and Gandhigram close to each other:

> It was in this curious circumstance, that one of Bhashkar's dreams was fulfilled: Steeltown began to move
> toward Gandhigram! (352)

Bhashkar himself joins the workers's procession and leads them towards Gandhigram so that Satyajit may be persuaded to break the fast. He fervently appeals to the assembled workers to stand by Gandhigram people for all time to come:

> One thing I must ask of you. Don't move away from Gandhigram – after the passion of the moment is spent. You will have to be with these people, always. Try to see what they stand for. Give them chance to understand what we are striving to attain. (356)

Thus both Bhashkar and Satyajit, as also Steeltown and Gandhigram, symbolizing the modern Western values and the traditional Eastern ways of life respectively, come close to each other. Both shed their rigidity and differences in order to coexist harmoniously.

Bhashkar's character itself is a curious mixture of the old and the new values. He has lived long in the West, but he does not forget his Indian heritage. Though he does not see any harm in drinking wine, dating and merry-making, he also has a high respect for the basic human values. For years Bhashkar has richly imbibed the American culture on the physical plane, yet he fails to attach himself spiritually to that culture and returns to India as soon as opportunity comes:

> He absorbed America with all his senses. Not know-how alone. He absorbed much of the human scene. He drank hard with the men. He dated with the women. He was now very far from his homeland – in something other than mileage. Yet it could well be that within him India remained as real as ever before, That, may be, was the reason why, even after a stay of twelve years, he could cut the strong pull of America all at once and fly back home. (35)

Rupa, a modern girl, half-American by birth, discovers to her disillusionment that Bhashkar has more of an Indian than of the Western man within him. She observes:

> So many years you lived in the West, absorbing its life, becoming part of that life. Yet back home, you were sucked at once into five thousand years of Indianism!. . . . The truth is that America as a whole has meant nothing to you. You brought back the industrial know-how. Not the know-how of life! This is the case with every Indian. He goes West and becomes a new person. He returns home and at once he is a complete Indian. (317)

What he loves in the Western civilization is its highly advanced scientific and technical knowledge. He wants, however, to introduce it in India to put the country on the path of material progress. For human values he is nevertheless drawn more to the East than to the West. This attitude of his mind also accounts for his preference for Sumita over Rupa.

Bhashkar's union with Sumita also illustrates a blending of the antagonistic values. In their marriage, Bhabani Bhattacharya synthesizes the Western with the Eastern elements in life. Bhashkar is a modern man, trained in America. He has absorbed the Western life-pattern with all his senses. He believes in living life as it comes to him. Completely "free in spirit" (122) he has not cared for traditional moral values. He has been concerned only with the physical pleasures: "His body had never thrived on asceticism. Where was the necessity." (122) Sometimes, he thinks himself a mechanical device that is unable to feel any thing: "Perhaps I am a kind of steel that can think. A computer. But I can't feel. That's it." (124) On the other hand, Sumita is a typical Indian girl of high ideals. Like her father, she too holds the traditional moral values in great esteem. She is "Indian of the epic age" (122) when compared to Rupa. She has deep faith in the Gandhian ideology. Simple living and high thinking form the core of her being. Pure at heart, she has not yielded to physical passions, though she is attracted towards Bhashkar. He is astounded when he finds her unmoved even by the sight of the erotic sculpture in the village temple:

> It was hard for him to believe that any woman could remain untouched by the sight of the hand on the breast, both so faithfully rendered. Sumita must have seen that sculpture many times in the course of years; yet, today, in the fullness of youth, how could she fail to see the reality she had missed before, and react appropriately? But there was her prompt dismissal of it with a click of her tongue. (127)

Sumita makes a profound impact on the Steeltown women by her simplicity and natural grace when she visits the Meadow House function. But in turn, she, too, catches the infection of the modern civilization at the show. She becomes conscious of the coarseness of her dress and bareness of her feet. Back home, she scrubs her feet with a piece of stone in order to make them look shapely. Further, she discards her white garb and wears a dark-green jacket and a green-bordered sari. She even adorns her forehead with a red mark and wears glass bangles. Thus she becomes "a changed person." (163) She begins to see her relations with Bhashkar in a new light. She knows that in order to live a happy married life with Bhashkar "Sumita would need a measure of orientation. It would be no easy passage from Gandhigram to Steeltown." (197) She feels happy when she notices a sudden change in Sumita and her attitude to Steeltown.

The married life of Satyajit and Suruchi embodies a synthesis of the old and the new values. Bhattacharya suggests the fusion of asceticism with worldliness in their marriage. Satyajit is a spiritualist. Worldly gains and physical pleasures have never meant much to him. He has been striving constantly for higher spiritual attainment:

> Material possessions had always meant little to him. It was inner satisfaction that had counted. He had been restless at Cambridge, shaken by storms within. At one time he had been obsessed by the idea of becoming a Buddhist monk and living in a monastic abode – in Ceylon may be, or Thailand.(14)

Back to India from Cambridge, Satyajit comes in contact with Tagore and is influenced by the poet's aesthetic ideas. He, too, starts believing that it is "fullness of life that makes one happy, not fullness of possessions." (14)

After some time, his marriage provides him with a complete "fullness" of life. Suruchi is a beautiful lady whose heart is brimful with love for him. They lead a happy marital life. But after some time, Satyajit meets Gandhi who summons him to take up constructive work at Sevagram. From that point, his transformation starts. He becomes more and more attached to the ideals of Gandhi and ultimately decides to lead the life of a celibate. He forces his decision on Suruchi also. Though Suruchi, out of her loyalty to her husband, yields to his wishes yet she is never able to reconcile herself to his ascetic view of life. The dull and monotonous life of Gandhigram irks her. At times she wants to revolt against him and Gandhigram. She sides with Jhanak when Satyajit wants to reprimand the girl for her betrayal of Gandhigram.

Suruchi, however, adopts herself considerably to Satyajit's wish. She becomes "part of Satyajit. The nail of his toe. A strand of hair on his scalp," (49) and realizes that Satyajit's ideals "had become part of herself. She was as much Gandhigram as he." (49) Yet, despite all this, the clash between the two contrasting forces – asceticism and worldliness – continues to disturb her mind. She is not able to accept or reject the ideals of Gandhigram totally.

Similarly Satyajit too, despite all his idealism and ascetism, is unable to subdue body. Occasionally, he has to gratify his basic physical urge. Morever, when Bires confesses his love for Suruchi to him, Satyajit is disillusioned. He cannot bear the thought of Suruchi going away from him. From now onwards, Satyajit starts "dreaming of a new life that she alone would fill." (212) He comes to realize how he has denied worldly pleasure to himself and Suruchi for long. In the light of this new vision, Satyajit tells her:

> "I will have everything that you condescend to give me, Ruchi."
>
> Surprised by his easy acquiescence she cried, "Condescend? Why do you say that?"
>
> "All these years I have deserved nothing from you, and yet my demands have been limitless. At last I see it all with clear sight." (341)

Suruchi will be the light of his life henceforth. He will let himself be led by her. He will fulfil her physically, and will himself be fulfilled by her. Satyajit reflects over their relations:

> Suruchi was an urge for him to live, relive . . . and not on the Gandhian plane. His newly won release would seek expression in the honest acceptance of every human need. (353)

Suruchi also realizes in her turn that during all the past years she herself has gained much on the spiritual plane. Now, she does not underestimate Satyajit's achievements on that level. All that she wishes is a synthesis of the ascetic and the worldly, of the idealist and the practical man in Satyajit:

> The past years, too, had brought enrichment, and she could not negate them, throw them away. And she would hate to see Satyajit cast himself adrift. She would like her husband to be Satyajit in one part of his being and someone else in another. That someone else – it was Bireswar! Yes, he could be both. That was the image in which she would want him. That was the image in which she could lose herself completely and be fulfilled. (341)

In this way, both Satyajit and Suruchi change. Both of them readjust their moral values, and create brighter prospects of a fulfilled life in future. Bhattacharya thus happily blends tradition with modernity in the union of Satyajit and Suruchi.

The synthesis of the idealistic and the realistic values of life is also signified in the friendship of Satyajit and Bireswar. The two friends are different in temperament as well as outward appearance. Although both are Cambridge-educated yet Satyajit has faith in the Gandhian philosophy, whereas Bireswar is a typically modern man who believes in the full enjoyment of pleasures of life. Suruchi notices the difference between the two friends:

> Strange that two close friends could be such worlds apart! Bireswar made mock of all Satyajit's beliefs. Even the spinning wheel drew barbed remarks. Satyajit in turn laughed at his friend. He said: Bires never means what he says. A queer fellow. You know, Suruchi, he never wore a hat in Cambridge, but as soon as he returned to India he bought one! (44)

While Satyajit is an epitome of the traditional Indian moral values, Bireswar flays such values. In this respect Bires comes closer to Bhashkar. He frankly admits to Satyajit:

> I have few inhibitions and fewer moral scruples. I firmly believe in getting what I need. (204)

Though Bireswar ridicules Satyajit's beliefs and ideals, he is much concerned about his friend's predicament – Gandhigram's threatened annexation by Steeltown. He raises his voice in the Parliament against the Government's decision to acquire the village, and makes them relent. He rushes to Gandhigram in order to persuade his friend to break his fast. When Satyajit refuses to oblige him, he feels very sad. Bhabani Bhattacharya's significant observation, "Life is all compromise. One yields a bit here and gets it back elsewhere," (115) sums up his synthetic attitude towards life in this novel.

II

Bhattacharya has developed his ideas of integration in *A Dream in Hawaii* also. The novelist projects here the view that there must be a blending of the old and the new values, the spiritualism of the East and the materialism of the West, in order to attain fulfilment in life.

Bhattacharya's intention to harmonize the values of the East and the West becomes evident to the reader by his setting the novel in the most Westernized island of Hawaii. The island presents "a multiple image" where one may visualize the "unique East-West mix. The strong interculturation."[3] The novelist observes: "You cannot find the like of this ethnic spectrum anywhere else on the globe." (56) In the opening chapter, Stella Gregson also states:

> Why . . . Hawaii? That's easy to answer, Swamiji. No better meeting ground of East and West. (12)

Swami Yogananda, the principal character of *A Dream in Hawaii*, is a Professor turned yogi. Although he preaches the spiritualism of the East, yet he also understands fully the Western value-pattern. Stella is convinced: "Within him the East and the West so readily coalesced." (18) He has nothing against modern science and technology. On the contrary, he thinks them essential for the progress and prosperity of the world:

> Unlike many faddists in the religious field Yogananda had great faith in technology. It was no longer a Western product, a Western challenge. All human society was set on being technology-based. This was a need for the preservation of life itself. (179-80)

But at the same time he realizes that science and technology help man only in the material progress. They are unable to give any spiritual help or guidance to humanity. A scientist who has no faith in the moral values can be a great danger to mankind. For these reasons, the Swami justifies the need of Vedantic spiritualism for the Western people:

> Science did not have the means to restrain itself—that was the problem. Restraint had to come from deep within the spirit of man. The spirit of man, which was beyond the intellectual level, was Vedanta's prime concern. (180)

Yogananda's ideas on the integration of diverse elements of life also find expression in his wish to install microphones and other modern gadgets in the Yoga centre under the big shady trees instead of the magnificent buildings.

He hates great walls that obstruct the free-mixing of different values and cultures. Although his main aim is to preach Vedanta in America, he is not apathetic to the problems of the American youth. He identifies himself with them:

> He ceased to be an alien. He merged himself in his listeners and they merged into him. He grew with them into depths of understanding, soul searching. They grew with him likewise. (179)

Swami Yogananda is a universalist whose character signifies a fusion of diverse cultures: "He belongs to America as much as to India." (197) Swami Yogananda also knows that an adequate knowledge of the material world is as significant for man as the profound spiritual wisdom. When Jennifer suggests that Swami Yogananda, the Eastern sage, may be an epitome of the spiritual wisdom, while Dr. Vincent Swift, the Western scholar, may represent the materialistic knowledge, Yogananda declares that the two are supplementary and complementary to each other: "There can be no true knowledge without wisdom, and no true wisdom without a hard core of knowledge." (201)

The Swami also knows that the proper adjustment of the two cultures plays a vital role in life. He does not adhere to his own ideas about the construction-plan of the Yoga Centre, but permits Dr. Vincent Swift to have his own way with some of the trees on the Centre site. Yogananda realizes:

> Some compromise had to be accepted. He had no wish to be rigid. Swami Yogananda justified himself. (209)

This attitude of compromise and readjustment helps Swami Yogananda a great deal in resolving the struggle of his own inner self, the struggle between the traditional Indian notions of asceticism or spiritualism and the modern Western conception of worldliness—Spirit and Body. He has himself experienced the conflict between these opposite forces from the very beginning of his career as a Professor of Philosophy. Though he renounces the world to live Vedanta in real life under the inspiration of Devjani, yet he finds it difficult to overcome his love for her. Sometimes he feels that his "release from his old self is final and complete," (12) but at times, he also yearns: "Why am I denied the plain lifeway of the common man?" (14) Consciously he strives to attain something lofty on the spiritual plane, but his sub-conscious mind occasionally revolts against such attempts, and forces him to make love to Devjani in his dream. Though when awake, he is ashamed of his infirmity, yet later he is "tempted to relive those moments with hate-love, while fighting to keep away" (44) her thought from his mind. For a long time, Yogananda lives in a make-believe world that having been reincarnated as a Yogi, he will have no desire left for physical love. But his belief proves to be a bubble in the air when Sylvia Koo dressed as Devjani induces him to make love to her in his sleep. He is ashamed of himself when he discovers his mistake. He realizes with a shock that the "episode was not meaningless, it was apparent. Pointed to a sickness deep down in himself." (229) He is now convinced that spirituality cannot be experienced by a man who is physically starved. In the wake of this knowledge, he makes a confession before Devjani:

> Swami Yogananda has ceased to exist. This man you see is Neeloy Mookherji. The yellow garb he still has to wear must be discarded. (232)

He further tells her that she has been haunting his dreams even during his stay in the Himalayan abode:

> At Sadhana, where I was so far away from your presence, you were in my dreams at night. Year after year. The truth is that I never got away from Neeloy.

By now, Yogananda has finally learnt that human life is not fulfilled merely on the ascetic plane; man must live life in its natural course, respecting all the fundamental urges. In other words, both Body and Spirit must be gratified equally in order to make life happy. As a consequence of this discernment, he decides to return from America to India where he hopes to lead the life of a common man, honestly accepting all the demands of body. Devjani understands his dilemma and approves his decision to leave America. When Stella asks her why Swami Yogananda called himself Neeloy while addressing her, Devjani makes a revealing reply: "'It may be that one cannot exist without the other,' she said." (245)

Walter Gregson, a typical Western man, also feels in the end that a fusion of body and spirit – sensuality and austerity – is essential for the healthy development of man. In the beginning, Walt represents the modern American man, having faith only in the materialistic values. He asserts: "He was the new America! He was America's today – and tomorrow." (197) Walt is a staunch votary of sexual permissiveness. He recognizes the "bed" as a key symbol for the new American, the American of the century's seventh decade." (24) He has no faith in high moral values of life, and firmly believes in the maxim: "Suck the juice and throw the peel away!" He fervently pleads for free sex and, as such, makes "no secret of his love affairs, posing as a liberated man and wanting even his students to adopt his so-called philosophy." (163) But despite his deep involvement in the sensual pleasures, Walt is not content within. His inner self agitates for something else than mere material possession or physical gratification. Gradually he comes to realize that it is not only his personal problem, but also a social crisis. He points out:

> The problem is: What now? You squeeze out the juice from life as if it were a bunch of grapes, and what's left in your hand is some skin, some seed, fit only to be tossed away. . . . The search cannot end there. You have to find something apart from the juice that's trickled through your fingers. Your need has become a crisis. (26)

His inner quest becomes so intense that it forces Walt to ask Stella to arrange his meeting with Swami Yogananda.

In the presence of the Swami, he vehemently defends the Western outlook about sexual permissiveness:

> The right to enjoy sex—that's normal. Abstinence—societal or self-imposed—that's abnormal. In our permissive society abstinence has no validity whatever. (59)

But the Swami at once observes that Walt is "obviously torn within despite his vehement self-assertion." (127) In course of time, Walt also becomes conscious of the raging conflict between two antagonistic forces within him. Like Devjani, he too, wants to "see all his own inner selves in a row," (199) just to ascertain what he hankers after. He has strange feelings for Devjani. On the one hand, she does not come up to his standards of a modern woman but, on the other hand, he is attracted towards the girl for her simplicity, modesty and chastity.

Though in a mood of desperation Walt sends his mistress, Sylvia Koo, to seduce Swami Yogananda, yet her success in corrupting the ascetic does not make him happy in the least. He is sorry for the fallen Swami, because in his fall is implied the defeat of high spiritual values which Walt has, of late, recognized in his inner self as essential for the Western man. Actually, Walt has identified himself, in a way, with the spiritual man of the East and as such, he feels that "Swami Yogananda's defeat was indeed a defeat of himself." (227)

There is a great change in his outlook now. Understanding dawns on him that life is not complete if lived merely on the physical plane, man must also have faith in the spiritual values which help him immensely in his inner crisis. In the light of this illumination, Walt decides to forsake his past way of life:

> One fact stood out. He had reached the end of his days with Sylvia. She had faithfully carried out the assigned task but that made no difference. (227)

Walt is thus convinced at last that he alone does not represent the American society of today in its entirety. Swami Yogananda, with his higher moral values, is also greatly significant for the materialistic Western social set-up:

> There was a new dream of youth, and Yogananda seemed somehow closer to that dream than he who claimed to be today's America. Yet he could not be rid of his urge for self-affirmation. He sat up in bed, thinking, and out of the chaos of contrary thought ways a strange conviction was taking shape: despite all his bitter challenge he himself was in deeply felt personal need of Swami Yogananda. (243-44)

Bhattacharya also pleads for a synthesis of the modern materialism of the West and the traditional spiritualism of the East through the character of Devjani in *A Dream in Hawaii.* In the beginning, he portrays Devjani as a typical Indian girl, having deep faith in the moral values of the East. Purity, modesty and simplicity make the core of her life, and she is terribly shocked to know about her mother's illicit love-affair. Her sense of regard for her mother is lost in the torrent of hatred. At that time, she is unable to comprehend the true meaning of her mother's remark, "constant self-denial is not my idea of life." (85) Disgusted, she leaves home for Benaras to carry on higher studies.

There is a tremendous void within her after the unhappy scene. In Professor Neeloy Mookherji, Devjani sees a potential *guru*, capable of helping her in her spiritual crisis. She induces him to renounce the world in order to lead a spiritual life and preach Vedanta to humanity. Devjani herself seeks anchorage in high spiritual values to fill her inner void. She discovers that "within her was a hunger for the spiritual life." (87) Denied the opportunity, she leaves for America and joins East-West Centre, Honolulu, for her research work. Free and easy life in the Western society gradually casts its impression on her mind. There is a broadening of her outlook now. She starts shedding her aversion of nudity, and when she goes to Waikiki Beach, she is almost charmed by the sight:

> it was the human scene that captivated her. The scantiness of clothes. She was both shocked and fascinated. Conceived in her

fancy, the view would have been repulsive; seen in actuality, it was only somewhat shameless. (98)

America begins to reshape her mental attitudes. She earnestly attempts to fit herself into the Western life-pattern. In reply to Alfred's question whether she wishes or not to be a part of the Western life-style while staying in America, Devjani asserts: "I do try." (81) Gradually, she comes to understand the reason behind her mother's action. Her talk with Walt is very revealing:

> And she spoke as if to herself. "I had no understanding. I was naive. So a molehill looked like a mountain. Even if it was really something very much bigger than a molehill."
>
> "Now the molehill looks its right size, I guess. How did that happen?"
>
> "I gained perspective. I gained respect for human needs." (198)

Even at this stage, Devjani is basically unchanged at heart. Though she starts recognizing the significance of the basic physical urges of man, the spiritual attributes still dominate her real self.

Devjani's leaving Hawaii for Harvard before Swami Yogananda's arrival there is, in a way, her acceptance of America. Yet her sudden and unexpected return, and taking initiation from the Swami symbolize her quest for spiritual values of life. In fact, there appears to be a conflict of ideologies within Devjani. She, too, experiences it and reflects: "She was as it were the Devjani of today and also of years ago, one as real as the other." (164-65)

Caught in this crisis of her inner self, Devjani fervently desires to have a fusion of Walt and Yogananda – the physical and spiritual attributes within her – so that her life may become meaningful. By now, she is able to conceive that her life cannot be wholesome without a blending of both these elements. Her self-introspection is significant:

> Let there be no misgivings, mused Devjani. It was in her American experience that she would find the values she searched for. All the same, she had to admit that in this hour with Swami Yogananda she was aware of an inner strength she had not felt before. (186)

The fact is that there is a see-saw of two contrasting forces in Devjani's mind. At times, she feels "an inner strength" in the company of Yogananda, while at other occasions, she finds her life's "bigger fragment merging into America." (187) She intensely desires to "see all my inner selves in some sort of mirror." (199) One day Swami Yogananda puts that "mirror" before her by declaring that he will be gone from America very shortly. Suddenly she realizes that "Yogananda gone, she would be unbearably alone. As alone as in those days in Varanasi when he had departed." (215) It appears to her that "all at once she was face to face – with herself." (215) And subsequently she declares:

> My place is in Sadhana. All else has become meaningless. Only Sadhana matters. (214)

At this juncture, Devjani establishes a close communion with Swami. When he tells her that Sadhana is only an "idea (that) can transcend its physical image and take shapes anywhere in the world," (214) Devjani tells him frankly: "Sadhana is you." (214) As a matter of fact, she is interested in Yogananda, the physical entity, and not in the values which he represents. She even pleads with the spiritualist for having a broad-minded approach to the Western way of life. She thinks: "To overreact to that lifeway is to lose one's perspective." (233-34) However, Devjani does not wish Swami Yogananda to become Neeloy Mookherji once again, and live life entirely on the physical plane, submerged in materialism:

> The thought came quickly upon her that he could not be two persons. What must he be? Yogananda or Neeloy? . . . Having become an illumined one, could he find fulfilment just as Neeloy? (234-35)

When Swami Yogananda forbids her to touch his feet because he does not deserve her salutation, Devjani answers him: "There is no Neeloy. . . . There is only Swami Yogananda." (242) She is, however, not sure whether Yogananda will be able to live a hermit's life, denying all the basic physical urges. She explains to Stella why Yogananda decided to leave America:

> "The ashram must possess him again, if possible." Her voice had a clear note of uncertainty. "If possible," she repeated. (245)

What Devjani ardently desires is a blending of the Western materialism and the Eastern spiritualism in the Swami. She will like to see in him both Yogananda and Neeloy integrated together, making him a complete man. She expresses her wish to him:

> "Reveal yourself again as an illumined one."
>
> With humility and reverence she touched her joined hands to the centre of her brow with its bright vermeil orb, but he who was filling her vision tumultously making her heart flutter wildly was Neeloy, just Neeloy. (245)

Another character of *A Dream in Hawaii,* Dr. Vincent Swift, is also a votary of the synthesis of the Eastern spiritualism and the Western materialism. Being "a romantic-realist, a down-to-earth visionary," (69) Dr. Swift always pleads for a compromise between the diverse values of life. He intends to establish a World Centre for Yogic Disciplines where Yogananda may preach Vedantic spiritualism to the Americans, yet he does not altogether ignore the prospect of material benefit from this centre and as such wants Yogananda's approval for his plan in toto. He believes in the give-and-take theory. He reasons:

> Swami Yogananda wants to Easternize us to a certain extent; in fairness, he should be ready to Westernize himself to the same extent. (129)

In his opinion, to stick rigidly to one's own ideas is never justified. One "must have a pragmatic attitude," (129) and be able to readjust one's values. He warns Swami Yogananda:

> Any attempt to Easternize all our Western concepts will be futile. We who seek success must accept certain limitations. Or else we shall find ourselves beating our wings in the void. (129)

What Dr. Swift seeks fervently is a fusion of different ideologies. He wants the World Centre to be based on this very concept:

> Vedanta was a color in his rainbow, and it was far from his intention to underrate that color. But it could not be the whole rainbow. The other colors had to be there. (144)

With his "idealism tempered by practicality," (69) he quickly decides to replace Yogananda, the spiritualist, with his own self when the man has left for India. But only in "one of his many dimensions he would have the persona of the Swami himself" (238); the remaining self of his will continues to be symbolic of the materialistic values of the modern Western society. In this way, Dr. Swift keenly desires to have an integration of the Western materialism and the Eastern spiritualism on the American land.

Thus Bhattacharya gives a subtle expression to his ideas regarding the integration of the traditional and the modern values – the Eastern spiritualism and the Western materialism in *A Dream in Hawaii.* The major characters emphasize its significance and attempt to mould their lives accordingly.

This critical analysis of Bhabani Bhattacharya's later novels amply illustrates the novelist's belief in the blending of the traditional and the modern values – the old and the new, Past and Present, feudalism and democracy, casteism and castelessness, affluence and poverty, spiritualism and materialism, asceticism and worldliness, the spinning wheel and the steel mill, East and West, and simplicity and sophistication. Each of his novels serves as a vehicle to project his concept of synthesis in the right perspective.

NOTES

1. Chandrasekharan, p. 107.
2. Bhabani Bhattacharya, *Shadow from Ladakh* (Delhi: Hind Pocket Books, 1966), p. 28.
3. Bhabani Bhattacharya, *A Dream in Hawaii*, p. 56.

The Short-Stories

Besides the novels, Bhabani Bhattacharya also has fifteen short-stories to his credit. Collected in *Steel Hawk and Other Stories,* they project a cross-section of life in India and abroad, and are concerned with a deeper emotional meaning, conveyed through their widely individual dramas. Since Bhattacharya is pre-occupied with certain other issues in these sketches, the theme of blending is not in evidence in all of them. In some of the stories, however, the writer does present a synthesis of the traditional and the modern values as well as the idealism and the realism.

Viewed symbolically, "The Acrobats" is a typical example of the blending of tradition and modernity. This story centres round two acrobats, the father and the "Boy." The father is old, mature and experienced, and embodies tradition in his nature, whereas the Boy is young and inexperienced, and represents modernity. Just as modernity is the offspring of tradition, similarly, the Boy is the child of the father acrobat. Both are supplementary and complementary to each other, and their life becomes a self-sufficient whole only when there is a complete harmony between them.

The father and the Boy live and perform their acrobatic feats together. Notwithstanding their relationship and difference in their age, they live like true companions, and there is a deep understanding between them. The father has undivided love for his child and the latter, too, has constant devotion to the former. Still there is a gap of age between the father and the Boy. The Boy is shocked and annoyed to see his father paying special attention to the young woman and neglecting him. The spirit of companionship between them disappears. The Boy grows silent and feels isolated, while the father remains engrossed in his own musings. In short, the old man and his offspring, the young boy, lose the harmony which existed between them earlier.

The Boy sees his father and the woman ogling together daily and, at last, he cannot tolerate it any longer. In order to show his unhappiness, he breaks the law of balance while performing upon the pole, and comes down with a thud. His right leg is broken. He is taken to hospital in an unconscious state. When he gains consciousness in the hospital, he finds his father caressing his legs. He tells him that the mishap took place because of that young woman standing in the balcony. The father can now understand "some of the pain, the protest, the ravaged feelings, the core of his son's inward storm."[1] There is a violent struggle in his mind, and at last, he decides to forsake the woman. Accompanied by the boy, he leaves the place for good. Thus he is again united with his son. Bhattacharya remarks:

> He sat with his face lowered, fighting his sore battle, stamping out a strident call of his blood and the warmth of a dream. With his strength of a lion, Father fought his battle.
>
> In the days and weeks that followed the young woman in the balcony stood leaning out over the brass rail for long spells, watching the bend of the street with tremulous expectation. She never saw the acrobats again. (99)

Actually this union of the father and the Boy signifies the synthesis of traditionalism and modernism. The story suggests that the blending of two polarities is a necessity for a smooth and harmonious living.

Another short-story, "The Quack," conveys the key-idea that human mind is prone to have faith in the traditional, the miraculous and the visionary things despite a deep awareness of the modern, the ordinary and the real facts of life. In other words, the author maintains here that the old and the new or the ideal and the real elements are synthesized in human nature.

The old man who meets the author in the audience, shows him his decaying teeth. Although he knows well that nothing can be done for his teeth because the dentist has already told him about it frankly, yet he is hoping against hope. His faith in the miraculous black powder, the so-called gift of a great yogi to the quack, makes him fall a prey to the quack and buy four packets of that powder. Describing the anomalous situation, Bhattacharya writes:

> An old man standing by my side, four packets tightly clutched in his fingers, turned his face to me with a grimace. "Look at my teeth," he pulled down his lower lip with his fingers to reveal the decay. Nothing can be done for them, the tooth-doctor says. True. What can you do with tree whose roots are gone? He caught my

> questioning glance on the packets he held and the grimace deepened. "All the same, as there is naught else to be done, why not hope a bit against all hope? Why not give every stupid thing an honest trial? Quackery? Yes. I am no trustful ass. But . . . what if it just happens to be otherwise this time? Just for once? Whoever can tell such things for sure?" (103-4)

Perhaps the most remarkable and the powerful story in the collection, "Steel Hawk," very emphatically highlights the blending of the old and the new, the ideal and the real elements in Indian life today. In this story, "Cart" signifies the old, considered ideal by people like old Grandma whereas the "Steel Hawk" stands for the modern that is very much real today. Grandma is the virtual symbol of synthesis. Since she is countless years old, she represents the old, traditional outlook of the past. But she is not altogether rigid in her attitude towards the modern times. She has always been a great admirer of the new inventions of modern science. In her early youth, she had felt immensely happy at the sight of a railway engine, and had exclaimed: "Truly, such a thing exists! To see this I must have earned merit by a hundred and one good deeds." (139)

This old lady is excited over the news of the Steel Hawk that has landed in the village pasture. She is as much anxious to know about the "flying wonder" as she had felt excited about the railway engine at the age of fourteen. Unable to move out because of gout, she asks her grandson, Bishan, to rush to the village pasture to have a good look at the Steel Hawk. Bishan acknowledges Grandma's curiosity about the wonders of modern science and technology: "Old Grandma, poor soul. Mad about tricky machines, stark mad! Same today as in her long-ago days, when the railroad first came this way!" (137) Grandma is thus not only of the past, but she has also got a spirit that readily accepts the present times. Bishan observes:

> Grandma could look at the flying wonder and go riding it in her fancy, zooming away mightily and shooting from sky to sky like a crazy star. Grandma had that sort of mind. She had it when she was young, and she still had it when her hair was without one black strand, all teeth gone, and sadness and pain written on her brow in each of the hundred wrinkles, graven deep. (142)

Bishan does not despise the old lady because, like him, she, too, has a natural bent towards modernity. This factor creates a deep understanding and perfect harmony between them. He broods: "Grandma's spirit was catching up with him! She who was of Yesterday was possessed by Today. Then how could one who was of Today be otherwise?" (142) Bishan sees in his fancy this "aged Grandma, with her modern dream, riding the Steel Hawk, soaring atop!" (143)

There is also a synthesis of the traditional and the modern elements in Bishan's character in the story. As a village cartman, he represents the old ways of life. But he does not adhere rigidly to the obsolete ideas and attitudes. The modern age has influenced his mind too. He fancies himself riding the aeroplane along with his Grandma. Commenting on his reveries, the author remarks:

> Impatient cow-bells tinkled into his reverie while he leaned against the fat, white flanks of an ox, but his neck remained craned, his mind remote. For the cartman of Sonamitti village had yielded to the impulse of the age and was riding the Steel Hawk with his Grandma, zooming away mightily. (143)

In the opening story, "Glory at Twilight," Bhattacharya brings to light the fact that human nature has a blending of the traditional and the modern elements: idealism and realism in it. Both these elements play a vital role in making human life a whole. Satyajit's character in the story embodies this idea. He shows the spirit of benevolence while deciding to help uncle Srinath even in his own lean times, and thus acts as an idealist. But at the same time, he is also well aware of the drab realities of life that he must face in future. Describing his predicament, Bhattacharya writes:

> Fallen from his castle in the clouds, Satyajit must tread the earthly ways of humble folk. But he could not deny the old man altogether. He must send some help. He had pondered over the amount. He had to ponder over each rupee before he spent it. (12)

The spirit of idealism makes Satyajit mortgage even his last remaining property for Srinath's sake. When the old man tells him that the village money-lender will advance a loan only after he has got Satyajit's house and pond as securities, Satyajit consents to do it despite his awareness of the danger involved in it. He tells Srinath: "Let the money-lender pay on those terms." (23) Satyajit, however, realizes the hardships he will have to face in future for he anxiously remarks: "What now?" (23) This is a question that is natural for every man who has a realistic attitude to life.

"Pictures in the Fire" is a story dealing with the psychological analysis of human nature. Bhabani Bhattacharya also uses it to express his ideas of integration. According to the author, dream elements and stark realities are closely woven together in the texture of man's life. Whenever the humdrum facts of the day-to-day life become oppressive to man, wishful thinking provides him with a respite, and temporarily diverts his attention. He wanders into a beautiful dream-world, and dreams of the good things of life. But after a short while, man descends on earth and is again ready to face the hard challenges of life with renewed zeal and replenished faith. The same process goes on continuously throughout his life.

The foreigner, who happens to meet the author in a slit-trench during the World War days, is worried and tired. The author sees "weariness in his white face, lines of strain plain enough in moonlight." (59) He considers the man as mad, thinking that the "war had torn his nerves and taken his senses. The frenzied look was unmistakable." (60) In fact, the man is very much disturbed and fatigued within because of the tremendous devastation and destruction caused by the war. Scared by the Japaneses air-attack on Calcutta, he takes cover in a trench to save his life, and has to pass an idle half hour. Fretted by the tenseness of the situation, he indulges in wishful thinking since he thinks that a "mad night like this is good for wishful thinking." (66) Wandering in his dream-world, the man idealizes himself. Fancy makes him a celebrated writer. But he has no wish to enjoy his success. He acts selflessly and all that he creates goes in the name of his wife, Josephine Brown, who becomes very popular. When the lady opposes it, he replies in the high sounding moral tone befitting an idealist:

> I enjoy this work, don't you see? That's good enough for me. Then there is an extra reward – it's exciting to see your name in print. One day, may be, I'II write something first rate. The critics will have many good things to say about Josephine Brown. Wait and you will see! (66)

But even in his dream, he is unable to see himself undermined or ignored. His feet still tread the solid earth of actuality. The inherent realism comes to surface. Since he, too, is a human being, he also aspires for fame and fortune. He thus makes a self-discovery and reflects: "He felt a great need of fame for himself. Perhaps that need had always been there, unknown and dormant. He had simply repressed it. Now it was going to torture him." (66)

As soon as the tense half-hour of the dark night passes, and the siren sings, "All clear!," he again becomes conscious of the real world around him. The author remarks:

> Our eyes met, he seemed at last to take notice of me. the sadness lifted quickly from his face and it broke into an amused smile. All at once he began to chuckle.
>
> "Picture in the fire!" he breathed. (67)

"A Moment of Eternity" is another story where Bhabani Bhattacharya presents the blending of idealism and realism—the two attributes of the traditional and the modern values. The heroine of this story, Mother of Sona-Mona, is a traditional Indian woman, completely devoted to her husband. She says: "I could bear the Seven Hells to give him the least relief. Oh, I could die a hundred deaths so he could be happy for a day." (77) None else matters for her besides him. When she comes to know of the fatal disease he is suffering from, she neglects even her children and devotes all her time and energy to his treatment. She lives on an idealistic plane, and thinks herself in terms of Savitri, the ideal wife, described in the ancient Hindu lore: "I felt Savitri in me, Savitri, who is ever in every woman. I could not be defeated, not unless I was lost, destroyed." (81) Drawing her strength from this belief, she untiringly looks after her ailing husband. When the dying man asks her to take good care of the girls after him, she firmly asserts: "We three have no existence apart from yours. In you we have three lives. In your dying we three die." (81)

In her bid to imitate Savitri of the ancient times, she first kills both of her baby girls and then attempts to commit suicide by eating opium. She is, however, rushed to hospital where she regains consciousness. It is "at this time that all images began to be sharp again in my mind. No madness was left. Sanity burned me." (83) Realities of life stare her in the face. She realizes what a heinous crime she has committed. As this sense dawns upon her, she faces her trial boldly, and is prepared to face her conviction gladly. While in jail, she realizes that there is no way to escape from life, and that she will have to live in this world, enduring all the pangs of the bitter memories of her past life:

> If not death, then madness, for that also could defeat memory. With each drop of my heart's blood, with each nerve and cell and sinew I prayed for madness. Sanity remained, a huge burning light in my brain. It gave vividness to all I saw with the eye within. It sharpened all I heard, to the least undertone of Sona-Mona's voices, their crying and laughing, their sniffing from a touch of cold and their deep quiet breathing in sleep. (84)

Thus, Bhabani Bhattacharya acts in his short stories also, as a builder of bridges between the two contrary, yet essential elements of life: tradition and modernity, and idealism and realism. He recognizes their dialectics, analyzes it, and then, suggests a synthesis of the two.

NOTE

1. Bhabani Bhattacharya, *Steel Hawk and Other Stories*, p. 99.

Craftsmanship

The study of a creative writer, howsoever exhaustive, remains incomplete and lop-sided unless he is viewed primarily as a craftsman. In other words, the tools in his smithy that help him in his work, viz. plot structure, characterization, form, technique of narration and language, etc., need also be discussed elaborately besides the themes he writes upon.

Bhabani Bhattacharya is also essentially a craftsman. Whenever his acute sensitivity makes his creative urge afire, and a peculiar theme strikes his mind, Bhattacharaya weaves the pattern of his story around it. In this process, he manipulates the plot, creates the characters and tells the story in his own way, handling the language so as to serve his specific purpose effectively.

Since the entire gamut of a story is covered by its plot, Bhattacharya takes considerable pains in knitting the plots of his novels. Being aware of the plot as "particular temporal synthesis effected by the writer of the elements of action, character and thoughts that constitute the matter of his invention,"[1] and also as a narrative of events in which the emphasis falls on causality,[2] he makes his plots compact, organic and economical. Instead of being loosely connected pieces of detachable harmony, his plots are well-knit and coherent. Nowhere does the novelist stuff his novels with irrelevant or incoherent material. The action of the story, in his case, advances its latent thought-content with the help of various characters. The characters, originally created to fit in the action-plan, affect and mould it in the course of its development, but are themselves also changed in turn by the events and incidents of the story. This is evident from characters like Kajoli, Rahoul, Mohini, Kalo, Chandra Lekha, Meera, Bhashkar, Sumita, Devjani, Walt and Jennifer etc. They have all been cast to project a particular point-of-view in the beginning, but as the respective plots develop and unfold gradually, all these characters respond to the new requirements of the situation, and reshape and readjust themselves in the process of changing the course of events.

Another significant feature of Bhattacharya's fiction is that his plots are based on the traditional pattern. Often with a definite beginning and ending, these plots have a sequential evolution. The time element plays a significant role in the development of his stories, and the whole action of the plot or sub-plot remains linked with time taken. Seldom does Bhattacharya allow the free-flowing of his characters's consciousness, disregarding the time-element and the sequential development of action in his stories. In his first novel, *So Many Hungers*, though Bhattacharya divides his plot into two strands, the story of the Basu family of Calcutta and that of the peasant family of Baruni, yet he puts them together in a proper time sequence to make them complementary parts of one single whole. The first sub-plot unfolds itself right at the time of the break-out of World War II and the birth of Rahoul's daughter. Developing with the passage of time, it finishes its course at the moment of Rahoul's landing in jail. Similarly, the second strand of the story has its beginning with the days of the Quit India movement. Covering the Bengal famine of 1943, it ends with Kajoli slapping the betel-woman and deciding to become a newspaper vendor in Calcutta until the lean time passes.

Bhattacharya's novels cover a number of events but they are not irrelevant in the story; there is a sufficient need and cause for each one of them to be included in the action of the novel. They effect the course of the story in their own way. But these effects are directly related to the basic theme of the novel. Thus Kajoli's rape by the soldier on the highway of Calcutta in *So Many Hungers*, Mohini's yielding to give her heart's blood to the goddess in *Music for Mohini*, Kalo's becoming a brothel-house agent and Chandra Lekha's rescue by him in *He Who Rides a Tiger*, the minstrel's giving an amulet to Meera in *A Goddess Named Gold*, Sumita's Delhi visit in *Shadow from Ladakh*, Devjani's flying away to Benaras from her house and Sylvia Koo's attempt to debase Swami Yogananda in *A Dream in Hawaii*, are but a few instances which, when analyzed critically, amply emphasize what E.M. Forster calls "causality" in a plot.

Bhattacharya's plots are generally simple. But he is also quite capable of weaving complex patterns for his stories. His *Shadow from Ladakh* is perhaps the best illustration of a traditional yet complex plot with various sub-plots and episodes which involve a number of characters.

The action of Bhattacharya's novels is often not a swift one. Slow and halting, it takes place, for the most part, in the minds of characters. In *Shadow from Ladakh* and *A Dream in Hawaii*, particularly, the narrative runs on two levels: external and internal. The external one deals with events on physical plane while internal one is concerned with the musings and reflections of the different characters and flows in their sub-conscious inner self.

The element of surprise or mystery to which E.M. Forster attaches great importance in a plot[3] is also present in each one of Bhattacharya's novels. Occasionally causing a shock, but generally giving an exciting turn to the course of events, this element not only keeps the readers's interest intact in the story, but also, being crucial to the development of the plot, leads to its final denouement. Every novel of Bhattacharya vividly illustrate the mysterious or the unexpected turn in the course of the events.

In *So Many Hungers*, Kajoli's decision to sell herself comes not only as a surprise but also as a shock to the reader who has known her as a brave and spirited girl so far. This momentary decision of the girl leading her to the betel-woman, and then, surprisingly enough, changing her mind and taking up the job of a newspaper vendor ultimately brings the story to a happy conclusion.

Similarly Mohini's sudden decision to offer her heart's blood to the Virgin Goddess in *Music for Mohini* stupefies the reader for a moment. He is at a loss to understand how a modern-minded and educated girl like Mohini agrees to bow to such a primitive practice. But later on the same incident forces Jayadev to come forward openly against his orthodox mother. A happy and perfect communion of Jayadev with Mohini – Bhattacharya's desired end of the novel – is possible only after this incident.

Chandra Lekha's abrupt decision to marry Motichand is another example of the similar element of surprise or mystery in *He Who Rides a Tiger*. Her decision shocks and bewilders not only the reader but also Kalo himself. It is this decision, however, that is immediately behind Kalo's bold action in exploding the temple myth before an elite gathering, and thus dismounting safely from the back of the roaring tiger of Brahminism.

The throwing of the amulet by Meera into the river in *A Goddess Named Gold* also creates a sense of suspense in the novel. Later on the same incident brings the novel to a convincing end.

In *Shadow from Ladakh*, at least two instances of the presence of the element of surprise and suspense may be quoted: firstly, Sumita's wearing of red lac bangles and a green bordered sari instead of the plain one after her return from the Meadow House show; and secondly, Bhashkar's sudden decision to lead the Steeltown workers's procession towards Gandhigram. Both these incidents are of a vital importance in the novel. The second one, in particular, is crucial to a happy close of the narrative.

A Dream in Hawaii also has similar surprising twists in its story. In the earlier part of the book, Yogananda's abrupt denial of Devjani's request for initiation against his inner wish creates a sense of mystery in the novel. Later on, Walt's sending of Sylvia Koo to seduce Yogananda in order to lower his prestige, and then, his unexpected shock and sorrow at the success of his plot and Yogananda's sudden decision to return to India give us good examples of the mystery-element in the novel. All these instances help the plot to develop and conclude convincingly by providing it the necessary turns and twists.

One major characteristic of Bhattacharya's plots is that though they tend to be tragic in the beginning, they finally end happily. Every crisis is resolved in the end, and the novels usually end with an atmosphere of calmness and serenity. Each of his novels has various sub-plots which serve as different episodes in a play. The characters are usually assigned their respective roles, and the situations arise out of the characters's development. These elements obviously point to the dramatic quality of his novels. Perhaps the most notable feature of all the novels of Bhattacharya is that they have a dramatic structure. All the major characters are generally introduced in the opening pages of his novels. The action in every story advances smoothly until it reaches the inevitable climax. Hereafter starts the anti-climax and the resolution of every crisis, leading to the end of the novel on a note of reconciliation and happiness. The conclusions of his novels correspond to Edwin Muir's conception of the end of a dramatic novel:

> The end of any dramatic novel will be a solution of the problem which sets the events moving; the particular action will have

> completed itself, bringing about an equilibrium, or issuing in some catastrophe which cannot be pursued farther. Equilibrium or death, these are the two ends towards which the dramatic novel moves.[4]

Bhattacharya's *So Many Hungers*, when viewed in this light, exemplifies that almost all the significant characters, viz. Rahoul, Kunal, Samaremdra, Devata, Kajoli, Mother, Monju and Onu, have been introduced in the opening pages, leading happy and peaceful lives in their respective places in society. As the plot unfolds and develops, there occur certain incidents and events affecting the lives of people, bad times of the Bengal famine, life of the destitutes on the road, Kunal's joining the army, the hectic days of the Quit India movement, and the bitter experiences of both Rahoul and Kajoli—the former suffering a lathi-blow on his leg and the latter being raped by a soldier. All these events inevitably lead to the crisis of the novel. Heavy blows fall on the heads of the characters; Kunal is reported missing in the battlefield, Rahoul is arrested for his anti-government activities, Kajoli decides to sell herself to the betel-woman in order to save her mother and younger brother from further misery, and last of all, Kajoli's mother, too, decides to commit suicide. This is the Aristotlian middle of the plot. But, with a view to saving the novel from lapsing into a tragic melodrama, the author resolves the crisis with the consummate skill of a master artist, and concludes the novel happily.

Music for Mohini also has a dramatic form. In the opening pages of the novel, Bhattacharya records Mohini's life at Shibpur. A little later, one sees Mohini's coming of age and her pangs of love. Jayadev is introduced in the plot at this juncture, and soon after he marries Mohini. The city-bred girl goes to Behula as the village-wed one. Living in her husband's house under the stern rule of her orthodox mother-in-law, Mohini has to suffer much. She has to change a lot in order to adjust herself to the wishes of the old lady. Still Mohini is unable to establish a harmonious relationship with her mother-in-law. This is the development of the plot so far. Then comes the crisis of the plot. Yielding to the ever-exacting and persuasive mother-in-law, Mohini is, at last, prepared to offer the blood of her bosom to the Virgin Goddess, and sets out for the temple with her old mother-in-law. When Jayadev comes to know of this awesome incident from Sudha, he immediately rushes to her rescue. He reaches the temple at the right moment, and Mohini is saved. The denouement of the action starts and all the loose strands are tied together convincingly. Mohini is discovered to be in the family way, and the old mother-in-law is very kind to her now. The discord between them ends and the novel concludes on a note of happiness and reconciliation.

He Who Rides a Tiger is another link in the chain of Bhattacharya's dramatic novels. Opening with Kalo and his daughter Chandra Lekha at Jharna, the plot of this novel gradually unfolds itself. Forced by the raging hunger in Bengal in 1943, Kalo has to leave Jharna for Calcutta. On his way, he is arrested for stealing and is sentenced to four months's jail where he befriends B-10 who tells him a trick to avenge himself on the cruel society. Having served his term in the jail, Kalo reaches Calcutta and tries to settle down in some respectable profession, but fails everywhere. At last, he becomes a procurer to a brothel-house. Seduced by the agent woman, Lekha too falls a prey to the same brothel where Kalo serves. She is providentially saved by him in the nick of time. Thereupon, Kalo plans to avenge himself on the society. He creates a fake Shiva. A big temple is built soon, and Kalo becomes twice-born as the temple priest. B-10 visits him after his release, and Lekha falls in love with him. Though Kalo is reincarnated as Mangal Adhikari, he is not happy and contented with his new life. Soon the course of the story takes an unexpected turn. Lekha who is deeply attached to the orphan foundling, Obhijit, agrees to marry Motichand whom she dislikes. This is a big jolt to Kalo. The story reaches its climax here. Suddenly the revelation dawns upon Kalo that if his daughter can sacrifice her life for his sake, why can't he? The story now heads for a convincing conclusion. Every move from now onwards is for the resolution of this crisis. Disillusioned by the realities of life, Kalo boldly faces the full throng of elite devotees and exposes the temple myth to be a lie. Having dismounted the tiger, Kalo leaves the temple on his own. He, thus, gets reconciled with Lekha, B-10 and Viswanath. Kalo was a blacksmith when the story commenced, and as it ends, we find him returning to his old job again. The cyclic motion of the story is complete in the end.

A Goddess Named Gold is also dramatic in its structure. The story opens with the Cowhouse women planning to lead a procession towards the Seth's shop in order to make him sell cloth at a fair price, but Lakshmi, the Seth's wife, is hesitant at the moment. Suddenly,

Nago, Lakshmi's only son, falls into a well and is rescued by Meera at the risk of her own life. Impressed deeply by Meera's courage, and out of gratitude for her, Lakshmi joins the procession and wins the battle for the village-women. The story develops smoothly from this point onwards. There are many turns in its course – the Seth's plan to deprive the village women of witnessing the cinema-show, Meera's ingenuity in sabotaging the show, the minstrel's arrival, his songs to entertain villagers, the "Taveez" trick, the Seth's discovery of the alchemic power of Meera's talisman, and his contract with her to share half of the gold produced by her – but the real crisis occurs when the touchstone proves troublesome instead of being a boon not only to the Seth and Meera, but also to the villagers . While the Seth has to suffer heavy losses on this account, the girl loses her reputation among the villagers who begin to consider her the scourge of the village. Atma Ram, the minstrel, arrives just in time to reveal the mystery of the amulet, and the novel concludes happily.

Bhattacharya's famous novel, *Shadow from Ladakh,* opens with Suruchi returning from the Peace Congress in Moscow. it is 1962 and China has treacherously attacked India. The country is in a state of shock and confusion. As the story unfolds itself further, Bhashkar Roy, the Chief Engineer of Steeltown, is shown planning to acquire the village pasture for the purpose of expanding Steeltown. Satyajit Roy, the moving spirit of Gandhigram, meets him in the meadow to dissuade him from acquiring the village pasture, but in vain. Bhashkar is impressed by Sumita's plain dress and serene looks, and there grows an intimacy between them. Bhashkar constructs the Meadow House, and a cultural function is organized there. Sumita watches the show and returns a bit transformed. Satyajit plans to take a Peace Mission to Ladakh, but is not allowed by the Government. To aggravate the crisis, Bhashkar gets the official permission to extend the frontier of Steeltown to include Gandhigram. Satyajit declares his fast unto death to make the Government rescind its orders. This provides the novel with its climactic point. The atmosphere in both Gandhigram and Steeltown becomes very tense. The explosive situation is calmed down by Bhashkar's timely decision to spare Gandhigram. He announces his improved plans to the assembled workers and then leads them on towards Gandhigram to make Satyajit break his fast. Suruchi and Sumita who have backed Satyajit also become reconciled with Bhashkar. Sumita meets him on the way and there emerges a new understanding between them. The novel ends with the suggestion of a happy communion between Bhashkar and Satyajit, Bhashkar and Sumita, and Satyajit and Suruchi as well.

A Dream in Hawaii is also conceived on the pattern of a dramatic novel. In the beginning, Swami Yogananda is shown at "Sadhana" – his Himalyan abode. Previously, he had been a Professor of Philosophy, named Neeloy Mookherjee, at Benaras University. In Benaras, he meets Devjani who has left her house in disgust because of the amorous affair of her mother, and joined the M.A. Philosophy class. Neeloy is charmed by her beauty, and Devjani, too, is deeply impressed by his learning. Later on, she becomes instrumental in turning the Professor into a Yogi. After completing her M.A. Devjani joins the East-West Centre, Honolulu, for her advanced studies in Philosophy. Inspired by Stella Gregson, Yogananda, too, goes to Hawaii with a mission to preach the Oriental Vedantism. But Devjani leaves Hawaii for Harvard before the Swami's arrival there.

The Swami lectures to a gathering of the University students, and the youngmen come under his spell soon. His disciples plan to establish a World Centre for Yogic Disciplines in Hawaii. The growing popularity of the Swami arouses the jealousy of Walter Gregson, a staunch votary of sexual permissiveness. He considers the Swami an obscurantist and a threat to the advanced civilization of America. He hatches a plan to debase the Indian mendicant morally through his beloved Sylvia Koo. Though the Swami escapes he realizes that in spite of all his penance and fasts, he has failed to overcome his love and passion for Devjani. He makes a clean breast of the whole incident to her, and immediately returns to his Himalayan abode in India. Bhattacharya thus hints in the novel at the conflict between the powerful pulls of the spirit and passion in human nature, or the dichotomy of essence and existence. Towards the end of the novel, the novelist subtly suggests that a synthesis of Body and Spirit is an essential requisite for a peaceful and prosperous life.

Bhattacharya's novels are thus dramatic in form, in which characters and plot act and react upon each other and advance the action to its inevitable conclusion.

II

Characters generally reflect the mind of their creator. E.M. Forster is of the view that the novelist "makes up a number of word-masses roughly describing himself . . . gives them names and sex, assigns them plausible gestures, and causes them to speak by the use of inverted commas, and perhaps to behave consistently. These word-masses are his characters."[5] Bhabani Bhattacharya, too, creates characters to represent his ideas.[6] In a way, his characters are more or less types, denoting certain ideas or values. Kajoli's father and mother in *So Many Hungers* have not been given any names. They simply stand for any and every father and mother. But this does not mean that Bhattacharya's characters lack individuality. The characters like Rahoul, Samarendra, Devata, Jayadev, B-10, Kalo, Kajoli, Lekha, Mohini, Heeralal, Meera, Sumita, Bhashkar, Satyajit, Devjani and Yogananda are highly individualized persons. Everyone of them can easily be recognized for his or her respective peculiar traits and qualities.

Bhattacharya is a novelist with a social purpose. He presents a realistic picture of the contemporary society, and hence his characters are bound to be real people. He frankly confesses to Sudhakar Joshi that most of his characters "have shaped themselves from the real earth."[7]

While writing a novel, Bhattacharya does not create characters before the invention of a story. On the contrary, he thinks of a theme and then introduces the characters and events according to the requirements of the plot. The development of character, in his case, is not in the hands of the author. His characters develop independently of the writer's intentions. Their personalities are influenced and moulded by the turns and twists of the plots. Bhattacharya reveals that "once I start writing, it is not I, but the characters and situations that compel me to be led by them. It is they who decide the way they should end. . . . Even the original plan [of a story] itself gets modified or changed due to certain traits which my characters develop during the course of events."[8]

Since Bhattacharya harps on the tradition-modernity theme, he creates some characters that are staunch traditionalists, upholding the old, established customs and beliefs despite their obsoleteness and irrelevance to modern times, and others that belong to the new generation, pleading for a change and a break from the outdated customs and conventions of the past that is dead and gone. As the novelist is of the opinion that life cannot be wholesome if lived only by any single set of values, and that there has to be a healthy synthesis of the two antagonistic yet essential value-patterns in life so as to make it happy and meaningful, he also creates at least some characters that virtually symbolize an integration of values. His Rahoul, Mohini, Jayadev, Rooplekha, Meera, Lakshmi and old Grandma are such figures.

Bhattacharya's novels also abound in characters that uphold a certain value-pattern in the beginning of their careers but change and readjust themselves to the requirement of the new times. They shed their rigid adherence to the old ideas and practices to a great extent, and also accommodate modern values as times passes. Examples of this type are Satyajit, Bhashkar, Sumita, Yogananda, Walt and Devjani, etc. Actually these are the characters that have some vitality. They are not mere cardboard figures or caricatures, but real living people.

Bhattacharya's characters can also be divided into two other kinds: those who symbolize certain values, such as Rahoul Devata, Kajoli, Jayadev, Mohini, Old Mother, the minstrel, Bhashkar, Satyajit, Yogananda, Walt and Dr. Vincent Swift, and the others who are objects of ridicule – mere caricatures – through whom the novelist intends to satirize and condemn the prevailing ills and evils of the contemporary society. Samarendra Basu in *So Many Hungers*, the priest of the Shiva temple in *Music for Mohini*, and the Seth in *A Goddess Named Gold*, are such caricatures.

A majority of Bhattacharya's characters are drawn from the middle-class society or from the peasant-and-worker community. His rustic characters particularly, have been portrayed realistically. Kajoli, her mother, Onu, Meera and her Grandma at once attract and impress the reader by their vitality, simplicity and nobility. They may sometimes appear simple or innocent, yet Bhattacharya treats them all with compassion, and thus preserves the readers's interest in them. But the exploiters like Sir Ablabandhu, Samarendra and the Seth of Sonamitti are pitilessly exposed. The novelist does not have any sympathy or liking for them.

Like Thomas Hardy, Bhattacharya excels in the treatment of his women characters. His male characters are often imperfectly delineated. Almost all of them are flat and two-dimensional. They hardly move or develop. Preconceived by the novelist, the male characters simply represent a single idea or value to which they adhere almost rigidly. Even if some development takes place, it is near the end of their careers, and is rather insignificant and almost invisible. They are more of types than individuals. Though the novelist occasionally attempts to individualize them, these male characters finish merely as algebraic symbols, quite unable to change and grow. Whether they are Rahoul, Kunal, Devata, Jayadev, Kalo, Satyajit, Bhashkar, Walt or Yogananda, the case is same with everyone.

Contrary to this, Bhattacharya's women characters are impressively drawn. They assume more significance than their counterpart male characters in Bhattacharya's fiction. Marlene Fisher, in her article on the women in Bhattacharya's novels, stresses that the most prominent factor in this novel is the importance of female characters, both as individuals and as symbols.[9]

Women in Bhattacharya's fiction are susceptible to changes that take place in the society. Old Grandma in the story, "Steel Hawk," is one such character. She is both of Yesterday and of Today. She can accept and acclaim the modern inventions like railway engine and aeroplane as unquestioningly as she has faith in the wisdom of *The Ramayana* and other scriptures. Meera's Grandma in *A Goddess Named Gold*, too, recognizes the significance of "Vote" in the democratic India, and is ready to play her part well in the changed times. This adaptability helps them develop in course of time. Hence they grow, act and react quite like actual human beings. They are not mere flat figures but living and round characters which cannot be summed up in a single phrase or a few words. The reader recollects them in the context of the great scenes they live through, the events they are involved in and are modified by. In fact, the reader comes to know about the contemporary realities as depicted in Bhattacharya's novels, more through the female characters than the male ones. Not only do they represent the novelist's ideas and ideal convincingly, but also speak for the Indian women as a whole. Kajoli in *So Many Hungers*, Mohini in *Music for Mohini*, Chandra Lekha in *He Who Rides a Tiger*, Meera and her Grandma in *A Goddess Named Gold*, Sumita and Suruchi in *Shadow from Ladakh* and Devjani in *A Dream in Hawaii*, are all prototypes of the Indian women placed in different situations of social life. While assessing Bhattacharya's characters, one observes that his heroines play a more vital role in the novel than his heroes.

Bhattacharya reveals a rare skill in analyzing the inner nature of his characters. The reader comes to know about his men and women more through their thoughts, inner conflicts, tensions and reactions than merely through their actions and appearances. Rahoul, Kalo and Meera are such characters as reveal themselves completely only through their peculiar broodings, mental tensions and struggles. But at times, Bhattacharya also resorts to other methods while delineating his characters. He makes his characters throw cross-light on each other through their conversation. At times he also intrudes upon the scene like an omniscient author and comments on their behaviour. With the exception of Jayadev who has an autobiographical touch of the author, Bhattacharya mostly remains detached, and never identifies himself with any of his characters. Lila Ray asserts that "Jayadev is the only one of his characters which bears an autobiographical resemblance to him."[10]

III

In matters of narrative technique, Bhattacharya uses both the conventional and the modern methods in fiction. As a true artist, he does not adhere to any single point of view for the presentation of his stories. Though he prefers, for the most part, to narrate the stories from the traditional omniscient point of view, yet at times he resorts to interior monologues to reveal the inner experiences of the characters. In his three novels, viz. *So Many Hungers*, *He Who Rides a Tiger* and *A Dream in Hawaii*, Bhattacharya makes experiment with this new technique of narration, though without exclusively depending on it. The reader becomes aware of the stream-of-consciousness of his characters: the flux of their mind, its continuity and yet its continuous change, as he happens to know of their silent musings or immediate thoughts or reactions to incidents. Rahoul in *So Many Hungers* and Kalo in *He Who Rides a Tiger*, are the characters who brood often, and their broodings reveal their immediate thoughts and reactions. The reader's communication with these characters takes place through their thoughts. Bhattacharya's last novel, *A Dream in Hawaii*, particularly opens with the musings of the protagonist, Yogananda. The internal monologue that takes place within Yogananda's mind at once illustrates to the reader what is passing in his mind. The reader is able to see things as

Yogananda sees them, and his thoughts are also identical with those of the hero. The writer does not try to intrude, and if he intervenes at all, he does it merely for the sake of a retrospective introduction of the hero and his surroundings. As one proceeds with the novel, Stella Gregson is found busy in Indianizing Jennifer's big living-room in order to receive Swami Yogananda. Her ideas, plans and recollections are all conveyed in such a way that the reader finds himself identifying with her and her experiences. Nowhere does he become conscious of the writer's presence in the narrative. The fact stands out that in this novel Bhattacharya frequently uses the stream-of-consciousness technique with its stress upon the interior monologue, though for artistic purposes, he mingles it with other conventional narrative methods, too.

In one of his short stories, "A Moment of Eternity," too, the stream-of-consciousness technique has been employed. The story opens at the moment when the heroine is standing in the court of justice, waiting for the decision to be announced. As soon as the judge starts reading the judgement, her thoughts fly back to her past life. The moment prolongs into eternity. An entire panorama of the bygone days with all the intricate details of happenings and incidents flashes before her inward eye at that moment. She does not remain conscious of her surroundings at all. The reader comes to know the true sequence only at the end. Before it, the whole narrative seems illogical and incoherent.

However, the stream-of-consciousness mode of narration, despite its successful use in *A Dream in Hawaii* and one or two more novels, is not his forte in general. He depends, to a larger extent, upon the traditional narrative methods. The stories in most of his novels are told from the neutral omniscient point-of-view. He enters into the hearts and minds of each one of his characters, and expresses their feelings and thoughts, adjusting them to their respective nature and temperament. In almost every book, one sees Bhattacharya introducing his characters, describing their peculiar traits in detail and sometimes even commenting upon certain happenings in the course of his narrative. Thus Kalo in *He Who Rides a Tiger* is introduced by the novelist from the point-of-view of the omniscient author. A number of incidents and occurrences that take place in this novel have also been either commented upon or reported by Bhattacharya from his own viewpoint. For this purpose, he uses the third-person narrative technique.

The novelist, for the sake of artistic success, quite often shifts the point-of-view from himself to a limited omniscient point-of-view of a single or a few characters. The writer, hiding his own individual self, either identifies himself with a single character, or projects his ideas through different characters. In Bhattacharya's case, various characters are individualized in each novel, and the story is told from their respective viewpoints. It is they, and not the novelist, who illumine the true nature of things in the contemporary society by revealing one another's characters and relating the happenings around them. Notwithstanding Bhattacharya's occasional intrusions in the course of narrative, the reader comes to know of the Bengal famine, the Quit India movement, the struggle, the miseries and the degradation of masses, fully through Rahoul, Kajoli and Devata as they talk with each other, and through their dialogues with other people in *So Many Hungers*. A major advantage of this method is that Bhattacharya as the omniscient and omnipresent author succeeds in unfolding before his readers comprehensive details about his characters and incidents in a logical, sequential and coherent narrative.

Another salient feature of Bhattacharya's narrative technique is the mode of telling the story "partly through recapitulation or reminiscence, or flash-backs."[11] Bhattacharya uses this technique in all his novels. He describes the situations or the turning-points in his characters's lives long after they actually took place. In *So Many Hungers*, Chapter Thirteen opens with Kajoli's family on the road leading to Calcutta and the novelist, instead of narrating the story further, takes a retrospective step to describe the circumstances in which they have left their home the previous day. Similarly, Rahoul is shown telephoning his father from the police custody, while the details of his arrest are disclosed later. In *Music for Mohini*, Mohini comes to know of Sudha's story in Chapter Eleven, but the reader is told in Chapter Thirteen what happens to Sudha a few months before Mohini's marriage with Jayadev. Chapter Twenty opening with Mohini riding a cart with her mother-in-law to the temple of Virgin Goddess records the happenings of the previous days that have finally culminated in the temple-visit. *He Who Rides a Tiger* presents another example of Bhattacharya's use of the flash-back technique. The reader does not get the details from Chandra Lekha's entry and distressing experience in the harlot-house in the chapter describing her rescue by Kalo. It is later on that she recapitulates her harrowing experience. In *A Goddess Named Gold*, the story of Nago's rescue from the well by Meera is narrated in the opening pages but her risky adventure inside the well is recounted in Chapter Twenty Seven. *Shadow from Ladakh*, too, provides a striking instance of Bhattacharya's use of the recapitulation technique. Sumita's going to the Meadow House, her slipping and the subsequent spraining of an ankle, Bhashkar's holding her tightly clasped against him and escorting her to her house, are all described earlier in Chapter Sixteen, whereas what Sumita feels at the moment of Bhashkar's hugging, and how she reacts, has been narrated later. In *A Dream in Hawaii*, the novelist relates the story of Professor Neeloy Mookherji turning Swami Yogananda in the opening chapter, but what happens to Devjani after his departure from Varanasi, and her reactions on being denied initiation by him, are not told immediately. The reader comes to know of these incidents only in Chapter Twelve when a long span of time has passed and Devjani is in America, brooding over her past. Once again in Chapter Seventeen, Devjani recalls to her mind the panorama of the past days at Varanasi, a state of loneliness and desolation, after Swami Yogananda suggests that in coming to America he committed a blunder, and that he should have been in India at that time, doing some constructive work for the society. Actually, Bhattacharya adopts the method of retrospective narration throughout this novel. The major characters of the novel, viz. Yogananda, Devjani, Stella and Jennifer, muse and recollect the events of their past.

Bhattacharya also employs myth as a part of his narrative technique in his fiction. At least one of Bhattacharya's novels, *Shadow from Ladakh*, exemplifies this. In this novel, Suruchi and Satyajit represent Sita and Gandhi, respectively. But Bhattacharya's use of myth is neither for digressional purposes (as found in Raja Rao's *Kanthapura*) nor as a structural device (as seen in R.K. Narayan's *The Man-Eater of Malgudi*). He takes up his mythical parallels simply to interpret certain situations or characters. One more peculiarity in Bhattacharya's treatment of myth is that he follows the mythical design to a certain point, and then, changes it completely, suggesting perhaps that the same ending is not relevant to the modern times. The novelist delineates Suruchi's character as the archetypal figure of Indian womanhood – the Sita image – in all her silent suffering and sacrifice. Though he has "reduced the Sita myth to its sexual level," yet "Kasturba has not been

Bhattacharya's mould in the creation of Suruchi"[12] as it may appear to some readers. The novelist does not wish to end Suruchi's career like Sita's and as such, the suggestion is made towards the end of the novel that her future life will be happy and fulfilled physically by her husband.

One of Bhattacharya's short-stories, "A Moment of Eternity," illustrates the use of the Savitri myth. The heroine of the story identifies herself with Savitri of the ancient Indian mythology. She thinks that like Savitri she, too, will not let her husband die an untimely death. But when the man succumbs to his fatal illness despite her best efforts, she also decides to end her life in order to accompany him to the other world. The writer has followed the mythical parallel upto this point only. To pursue it any further does not seem plausible to him, and he altogether changes the course of the events that take place further in the narrative. The woman is apprehended and sued for an attempted suicide and the murder of her girls. Sentenced to four years's rigorous imprisonment, she remains alive, constantly haunted by the memory of her dead husband and children.

IV

Bhattacharya has made an impressive use of symbolism in his fiction. This device not only successfully conveys the changing patterns and variegated shades of life in the contemporary society, but also provides the novels with multiple and deeper meanings. Besides the characters who represent certain ideas and ideals, there are some situations, gestures, plants, songs and animals that suggest something beyond their literal meanings. The very title of *So Many Hungers* is symbolic, suggesting the nature of hungers – for food, freedom, fortune and flesh – that pervaded the land of Bengal in 1942-43. There are also a number of other significant symbols inside the story. For instance, Kajoli's cooing like a Kokil signifies her happiness, the Madhobi vine arching the station gate when in full bloom, suggests the richness and affluence of Bengal, whereas the same vine when dry and withered, stands for adversity and dreariness in the land. Vultures and jackals are symbolic of man's cruelty and ruthlessness besides being mere birds of prey or beasts. The songs introduced in the novel also have symbolic meanings.

Music for Mohini abounds in symbols. The Big House stands for tradition, hyacinth in the temple-pond is symbolic of the evil growth in society, whereas its uprooting by Harindra and others signifies the youth's revolt against the prevailing social evils. Mohini's coming out in the garden and sitting on a tree-perch reflect the defiance of the social authority by the younger generation. Mohini's breaking of her dilruba also embodies the protest of the youth against the unnecessary restraints imposed on them by the old folk. In *He Who Rides a Tiger*, Kalo's setting up of a smithy even while acting as Mangal Adhikari signifies that he is still Kalo the "Kamar" from within. Lekha's fierce reaction at B-10's attempt to embrace her is emblematic of a woman's repulsion from a man's mere physical passion. The temple itself is a symbol of falsehood in religion. Similarly, Lekha's decision to marry Motichand, and Kalo's bold act of exploding the temple myth are symbolic acts denoting much more than their apparent meanings.

A Goddess Named Gold is an extended allegory in which symbolism has been used as the basic pattern of the whole story. Gold itself is a symbol with multiple meanings. It can be interpreted both as the material and the spiritual wealth. As the material wealth, it denotes both power and possession. But as the spiritual wealth, gold symbolizes purity of soul and goodness of character. The touchstone is another symbol, epitomizing India's national freedom. The acts of kindness which the minstrel refers to are the symbolic acts of faith and reconstruction in independent India. There are two more symbols, one of them being a spider ensnaring a red ant in its web under the trunk of an uprooted and dry tree. The Seth watches the insect with keen interest. He identifies himself with the spider. Both entrap and destroy their victims. Hence, he has a core of sympathy for the spider. Another symbol, referring to the cruel exploiters of the rural society always ready to suck the blood of the masses, is a snake which has half-swallowed a frog. The symbol implies that the poor rural people are as helpless before the cruel money-lenders as the frog in the clutches of the vicious snake.

Two symbols that stand out prominently in *Shadow from Ladakh* are Steeltown and Gandhigram. Apart from their respective physical entities, both of these represent two distinct ideologies and ways of life. Gandhigram is an epitome of the Gandhian idea of rural economics in which self-sufficiency is to be achieved through cottage-industries. It also stands for India's rich cultural past with all the long-established traditions and high moral values. Steeltown, on the other hand, is emblematic of heavy industries for the country. It also symbolizes the modern technological age which has no regard for Gandhigram type of values or traditions. The conflict between Steeltown and Gandhigram is not only a conflict between the economics of cottage-industries and industrialization but also between the spiritual and material values of life. Suruchi's breaking of her bangles is also a symbolic gesture, suggesting the repression of her physical passion. In the same way, there are other symbolic situations or actions in the novel that add to the meaningful interpretation of its theme.

Symbolism in *A Dream in Hawaii* is, for the most part, inherent in its characters. All the men and women who figure in the novel are types, representing ideas and sets of values. Apart from these persons, Bhattacharya takes up certain situations and actions that are also symbolic in nature. For instance, Yogananda's love-making in dream is indicative of the fact that the genuine and natural demands of body cannot be suppressed completely. Perhaps the only symbol that Walt mentions in the novel is "the bed," signifying the temperament of the American youth in the seventies. It characterizes in general an abnormal bent of the modern Western man towards sexual revelries.

The steel hawk and the ox-cart stand out as the prominent symbols in the story, "Steel Hawk." The former is representative of the modern age and machine, whereas the latter signifies the old age. The steel hawk is of today, while the ox-cart is of yesterday. They are also symbolic of the Western and the Eastern values of life respectively.

V

Among various stylistic devices that Bhattacharya employs in his fiction are irony and humour. The novelist uses irony effectively. With the help of this device, he throws an illuminating light upon some peculiar aspects of his characters or exemplifies the unreality or absurdity of certain situations. Two striking instances of Bhattacharya's use of irony can clearly be visualized in *So Many Hungers*. At one place in the novel, Monju asks her hoarder father-in-law, Samarendra Basu, to give a cheque so that her husband may buy rice from the black market in order to feed the hungry destitute. Samarendra signs the cheque, but in his heart of hearts he contemplates that "some of this amount would return to him via the black market and its intermediaries working up to Cheap Rice, Ltd." (180) Another example is in evidence when a desperate Kajoli decides to sell herself at the brothel-house, and takes eighty rupees in advance from the betel-woman so as to enable her mother and younger brother to survive. But the same night, her mother, too, decides to commit suicide because she is unable to see her children hungry any more. Again, the mother wraps her body, while going to drown herself in the Ganges, with a gunny-sack. Kajoli has tied in a corner of this sack all her ill-earned amount. The ironical fact stands out that this money can save none.

In *Music for Mohini*, Bhattacharya uses irony to describe the absurdity of situations, and meanness and revengeful attitude of man towards man. The novelist narrates how a bride-showing ceremony takes place at Mohini's parental home. The party consists of uncultured and indecent lot who examine the girl physically, rubbing her cheeks, pulling her hair down and baring her legs upto knees. This thing enrages the Professor who turns them out of the house. The irony is that while leaving Mohini's house, the old man of the party calls to her people: "Come away, . . . This is no place for gentlefolk." (42) Another example of irony is in Sudha's views about Mohini. Sudha thinks Jayadev's bride as her rival. She earnestly wishes Mohini to remain barren so that Jayadev's mother may turn her out of the Big House, replacing her with Sudha. With these thoughts in her mind, she tells Jayadev about Mohini's temple visit. Totally unaware of Sudha's malicious intentions, Jayadev is grateful to her for the information. As he does not believe in the prediction of the horoscope, he immediately rushes to the temple and saves his wife in time. The end of the novel also supplies with an instance of irony. Bhattacharya tells here that Mohini's pregnancy declared, her future is secure and bright at the Big House. That is the end of every discord with her mother-in-law. Accompanied by Jayadev, she sets out for Shibpur to visit her parents. As Sudha sees from a window, the palanquins carrying them pass her house, she rejoices thinking that Mohini has been discarded and she will soon replace her as the mistress. The fact is that there is no chance for her now and that she lives in a fool's paradise.

Irony is also in evidence in *He Who Rides a Tiger*. The reader at once becomes aware of it when Kalo, working as the agent of a brothel-house, greets and shows the way to a visitor (66) without knowing that his own daughter, Lekha, is going to be a victim of the same rich man that night. Again, the novelist employs irony in the account he gives of the inconsiderate magistrate touching the feet of the imposter Kalo and seeking his benediction. The novel records:

> He paused, with a sudden amused look. His voice changed, "Yesterday a man came and touched my feet humbly Lekha, he was no other than the magistrate who sent me to prison, the magistrate who asked, 'Why do you have to live? Why does your daughter have to live?'" (92)

One more instance of irony in *He Who Rides a Tiger* occurs when Viswanath addresses Kalo: "So long as there are true-hearted Brahmins like you, people cannot lose faith in this social order." (122) The fact is that Kalo is neither true-hearted, nor a Brahmin.

There is enough scope for the use of irony in *A Goddess Named Gold* since the novel has satirical overtones. The irony in this novel is mild as well as bitter, depending largely upon the situation or the character. A good example of mild irony is found in the Seth's abnormal use of his silken umbrella. Instead of protecting himself from heat or rain with its help, he protects the umbrella itself against the hard sun. When Bulaki Rao asks the Seth to open it, he bluntly refuses, saying: "What! The sun is still strong, you cannot see?" (38) Again, there is an ironic constrast in the Seth's words and deeds. The reader is amused to hear him tell the minstrel:

> Ho, minstrel if only you knew! I care as little as you for worldly goods. People do not understand me. They do not see that I collect money for their benefit. It goes to them as loans without which the newborn will not hear the priestly chant, the marriage music will ring hollow, the dead will be denied the last ritual. Life itself will stop. (72)

The minstrel's remark in reply, "Seth Ji, yours is a dedicated life," is ironical, but the Seth fails to comprehend it Bitter irony is implied in the Seth's gesture of generosity towards his victims whom he dispossess every now and then. The novelist comments:

> Who would complain that the Seth had acted harshly without human feeling? Every man who migrated in distress received a cash gift from him. Five rupees, ten rupees, or even fifteen, depending on the acreage he had lost. There were no real grounds for such a gift. You bought wheat and ate it, you bought cloth and used it up – the dealer would not make a free replacement of even one grain or one strand of thread – but the Seth of Sonamitti was too soft in his dealings. That was his trouble. (132)

The irony of situation is implicit in the Seth's various attempts to make Meera do the acts of kindness in order to make the amulet work. In one such bid, he tries his best to get a drunken man married to the Bad Woman of Pipli to bring about their rehabilitation and reformation. But contrary to his intentions, the Seth fails to reform either of them. The drunkard continues to drink with his friends, and the Bad Woman goes on plying her trade of prostitution right upto the proposed hour of the marriage-ceremony. Even Bulaki Rao, the priest called to solemnize the marriage, is busy in counting the money he has received as his commission for procuring customers to the woman. The helpless Seth has to make a hasty retreat from such a place.

Irony is used as a significant device in *Shadow from Ladakh* to highlight the polarities of Steeltown and Gandhigram. Most of the important events in the story such as Sumita's visit to Delhi or Bhashkar's attempt to annex Gandhigram in Steeltown have ironical results. The author uses irony to expose affectations of characters also. The episode describing the Meadow House function (Chapter Seventeen) is an the example in point. Two ladies are very eager to hook Bhashkar as groom for their daughters. When he plans the function at the Meadow House, both the ladies take it as the most appropriate opportunity to show the girls to him. While preparing for it, they altogether change the programme, defeating Bhashkar's intentions, and make the function a Lohapur Club cultural show. In fact, Bhashkar wants it to be a get-together of both the millhands and the Gandhigram people. The irony is that despite the frantic attempts by these ladies, Bhashkar does not take the least interest in either of the gaily-dressed dancing girls. Instead, he is fascinated by the white-garbed and barefooted Sumita.

Similarly irony is unmistakably used by the novelist in Chapter Thirty One. The Deputy General Manager's wife (Number Two) tries her best to appease Muthuswami so that he may send to the press a detailed report and the photograph of Lotika donating her ornaments. But the man "wore an air of studied indifference" (276) despite her attempts.

A Dream in Hawaii contains examples of both the verbal and situational irony. The verbal irony is revealed through the subtle utterances of Swami Yogananda who discerns a wide gap between the intentions and actions of Dr. Vincent Swift described as "culture-vulture." The situational irony is used to deflate the Western sensuality by juxtaposing it with the Eastern spiritualism. It is ironical that Walter Gregson who is against the Swami, feels unhappy when the later leaves Hawaii. He, a votary of sexual permissiveness, cannot bear the thought of Yogananda preaching the Eastern spiritualism to the American youth, and thus distracting them from the free and easy life-ways of the West. He sends his mistress Sylvia to seduce the Swami. The woman is partly successful in her attempt as she discerns the Swami's secret and repressed feelings of love for Devjani. Walt has been eagerly waiting for the news of her success but, ironically, when he comes to know of Yogananda's fall, he takes it as his own defeat, in a way. Hence he discards the companionship of Sylvia Koo for ever. Describing his feelings, the author remarks, "And the bitter cry was raging within him. To hell with it all, to hell with it all." (227)

Irony is used as a favourite device by Bhattacharya to expose the incongruities in the nature of characters who reveal a wide divergence in what they profess and what they do. This is particularly evident in his short-stories. In the opening story, "Glory at Twilight," Satyajit is fully conscious of his ruin, yet he goes out to the extreme end in helping Uncle Srinath and even mortgages his last bits of property – his house and pond. The irony is that having taken such a bold step knowingly, he asks himself: "What now?" as if all this happened without his knowledge.

In the story, "Public Figure," the writer satirizes the hypocrisy and craze for publicity among some people who pose to be public men. The hero P.F. invites Muthuswami, the local press correspondent, to his house, and serves him with sweets and tea. The sole purpose behind this courtesy is that he wants the photograph of his daughter, Nolini, at the time of donating her ornaments to the Defence Fund to be sent to the newspaper for being printed. But the man is not much impressed by the idea and does not agree to send the photograph to the newspaper he represents. Even the news that appears in the newspaper is brief and insignificant. P.F.'s face is clouded at it, and he broods: "That Muthuswami rat! That rat would have to be chastised—hard. There were ways—and ways. In good time—in good time. . . . All in good time." (32)

In "The Quack," the old man who buys four packets of the black powder from the quack, has already been plainly told by the dentist about the helpless state of his teeth. The irony is that he believes that road-side quack despite knowing that such persons are very deceitful. Bhattacharya observes:

> All the same, as there is naught else to be done, why not hope a bit against all hope? Why not give every stupid thing an honest trial? Quackery? Yes, I am no trustful ass. But . . . what if it just happens to be otherwise this time? Just for once? Whoever can tell such things for sure? (104)

Besides irony, Bhattacharya is also gifted with a rich sense of humour. He may occasionally tinge the serious flowing narrative with a tone of lightness, thus relieving the reader of the looming tragedy, and making him laugh at the incongruities of the situations or characters. K.R. Chandrasekharan opines that Bhattacharya's humour "usually arises from a perception of contrasts—the contrast between the appearance and the reality or between what is and what ought to be. In other words, his humour is both relative and absolute."[13]

In *So Many Hungers*, the reader is amused to know Samarendra's reactions at the sudden arrival of a police officer at his house. At first, he is horrified at the thought of Rahoul's apprehension by the Police: "Pale, struck dumb, Samarendra clutched the arms of his chair. Dryness spread fast over his palate, with grim pictures forming his fancy. The house being searched. Rahoul arrested. It was Rahoul, of course, for he had gone down to the village, involved himself in some act against his Emperor." (30) But as soon as he comes to know of the officer's arrival from the Government House, he assumes arrogant airs, feeling proud of the same Rahoul. Describing the humorous situation, Bhattacharya writes:

> Rahoul was leaving the room when the visitor appeared, but his father lifted a hand to his shoulder, introducing, proudly showing him off: "Dr. Rahoul Basu, my eldest son. D.Sc. of Cambridge University." And suddenly, to the amazement of the visitor, he broke into a chuckle, his face shining with a joy he could not hold. (31)

Music for Mohini presents several examples of humour. The very first chapter of the novel, describing the happy and care-free life of Mohini and her brother Heeralal in Calcutta, provides good amusement to the readers. Disturbed by their childlike mischiefs when the Professor enters the children's room, he finds both of them seriously engaged in studies. On being checked, the book lying open before Mohini is found to be a pornographic novel instead of a history book, and Heeralal's pencil with which he feigns to do arithmetic has no point. Further, the Old Mother's unnecessary restraints upon the growing children and their novel way of countering the same are very humorous. The children are required to observe certain norms while seeing a movie with a love-scene. Heeralal is supposed to shut his eyes tight, whereas Mohini is to cover her eyes and her face with one end of her sari. Both the children follow the instructions apparently. But there is "no effect on Heeralal who had trained himself to see clearly through half-closed eyes." (31)

There is a subtle humour in the clever excuse given by Mohini to escape the ordeal of getting his nose pierced for holding a bright diamond ring in it. She humours her superstitious mother by saying that her nose has been dedicated to the goddess Kali in her childhood. It will arouse the wrath of the goddess if it is pierced.

He Who Rides a Tiger exemplifies Bhattacharya's use of sardonic humour in the unhappy experience of young Chandra Lekha as the priestess of the Shiva temple. The rich stock-broker, Motichand, sees in Lekha "the very image of Gauri, the great god's spouse in heaven. (89) He asks her whether he should buy or sell shares that day. Lekha, knowing nothing about the share business, is utterly confounded. In her state of confusion, she simply repeats the words "buy" and "sell" as she has heard from Motichand. Taking her words as the godly advice, he acts accordingly and makes huge profits. Thus his faith in the fake Shiva becomes firm.

A Goddess Named Gold provides much scope for humour. Experimenting with a new technique and style, the novelist exhibits his unique sense of humour in this novel. As Chandrasekharan points out, Bhattacharya has "a mischievious dig"[14] at husbands and schoolmasters. Out of their plight, he brings out humour in this novel. A typical scene describing the confrontation of two groups of processionists, one comprising the village women and the other the village school-boys with their Master-ji, gives rise to a humorous situation. Describing the funny situation, the novelist writes:

> The two columns surveyed each other, the boys alarmed and the women scornful, and then an odd thing happened. Master-ji spun round, facing the youngsters.
>
> "Dismiss!" – and he was in swift flight.
>
> "You saw?" Master-Ji's hefty wife beamed at the procession, her arms on her hips.
>
> "Because of you he fled?" asked Sohagi in surprise.
>
> "What else?"
>
> "Sister," Sohagi was wistful, "all husbands should be just as brave as yours." And she turned to Lakshmi as if to say, "you will agree." (127)

Sometimes the novelist picks up a character, and arouses humour through his thoughts of actions. The Seth in this novel is one such person. He has curious thoughts in his mind:

> A New thought struck him, a regret. If only Nago were elder, a grown-up lad, and Meera could be wed to him. To have her for his son's wife. The sadness that Nago was born so very late. His mother came late into this household and then took full three years to conceive. (143-44)

The Seth can also be witty at times. His asking Bulaki Rao to leave the place for an hour in order to avoid the chances of eavesdropping, is amusing:

> "Go away," he exploded. "Take a lone walk in the meadow."
>
> "The heat!" Bulaki Rao moaned. "Even the meadow grass is scorched, not one green blade left."
>
> "Indeed! Then what will you eat?"

"Ji?"
"Move off. Stay away for an hour."(144)

The Seth is the chief source of humour in *A Goddess Named Gold*. As soon as he signs a contract with Meera, he sends a letter to the local newspaper, giving a detailed account of the touchstone story. When the letter is printed in the paper, he sits at his city-shop, expecting people to come to inquire about the authenticity of the news. But no one in the city seems to care for the touchstone story. He broods unhappily:

> An evil day in every sense. Would that he had not come to town when there was so much to be done at Sonamitti. Why had be bothered about city gnats? The touchstone would gain nothing from them, or lose. (188)

The Seth's frantic attempt to do the acts of kindness are also very humorous.

The novel, *Shadow from Ladakh*, contains a number of instances that arouse humour. While going through Chapter Eight of the novel, the reader is amused to observe Great-Uncle holding a letter before Sumita's eyes. He wants Sumita to close her ears so that she is not able to hear what she reads before him. The simplicity of the Great-Uncle arouses laughter:

> "Let me read it out."
> "Wait. Private letter, this, understand? Not for your hearing. First clap your forefingers to your ears – hard – so that no word can get in. Hold the fingers pressed hard." He indicated the way. "So . . . :"
> Catching the idea, she broke into laughter. But stopped herself quickly. Her hands went up, obeying, to her ears.
> "What now? The letter? Have I three hands, Great-Uncle?"
> "I will hold each sheet before your face. So . . . .!" He peered, making sure her ears were closed, then gestured to her to proceed. A minute's reading brought Sumita to the core of the letter. (75)

Similarly, Chapter Ten of the novel opens with an interesting dialogue between Great-Uncle and the messenger-boy from Steeltown. Despite the latter's repeated protestations that he is not a postman, the old man goes on addressing him as the new postman of Gandhigram:

> Great-Uncle was beaming at the youngster. "What has happened to our postman Radhanath? May be he is cancelled, like a used stamp!"
>
> "I'm not a postman. I told you." The boy made a face again.
>
> Great-Uncle nodded to himself. "A different kind. One in blue coat – pentaloon, like a saheb. Times are changing."
>
> "Haven't I told you already – "
>
> Sumita intervened. "Great-Uncle will you help this boy deliver his letters? He's a stranger in this place."
>
> "I will, if postman-brother wants my help."
>
> The boy blinked in anger. "The fourth time!"
>
> Sumita tried to appease him. (84-85)

The cultural conflict provides the novel, *A Dream in Hawaii*, with a fertile ground for comedy. Humour in the novel ranges from subtle to the crude one. Whenever the novelist wants simply to amuse his readers without ridiculing a particular character or situation, his humour is subtle. For instance, Swami Yogananda, though quite young, declares himself to be hundred years old. When Dr. Vincent Swift asks him his age, the Swami humorously replies that it was his "hundredth birthday." (16) The reader is greatly amused at the reply but he does not condemn Yogananda for his overstatement when he considers the context in which Yogananda calls his birthday "hundredth." He, though amused, is well-satisfied with the authenticity of the reply.

Occasionally, Bhattacharya's humour also becomes sardonic in this novel. The episode where a young Amercian woman, Frieda, invites the Swami to copulate with her, calling it "heaven's ambrosia" (111) or *Amrita*, is very interesting and amusing. The reader laughs at her abrupt attempt to seduce the Swami and her bitter disappointment at her failure. The novelist makes fun of the Western concept that copulation is the only supreme bliss for man, and that no one can resist the desire for sex when given a chance. Yogananda remains indifferent to Frieda's open invitation to have sex with her. Her disappointment and disgust arouse the reader's laughter.

Bhattacharya's short-stories also abound in humour. There are a number of instances in these stories which arouse laughter. "My Brave

Great-Uncle" is a story written entirely in a lighter vein. Great-Uncle's tales about ghosts, gnomes, spooks and other spirits, and his novel way of clapping hands to ward these evil spirits off are greatly amusing. Finally, his fear of ghosts presents a hilarious scene in the story.

In "Lattu Ram's Adventure," Bhattacharya deliberately satirizes people's tendency to display wrong English signboards at public places. Lattu Ram happens to see a signboard that reads like "LADY SHOES." Another one reads "ORDER SUPPLIERS PROMPTLY EXECUTED." A third one proclaims: "SEATS OF CUSTOMERS PROPERLY CANED." Still another exhibits: "DO NOT SPIT ON PUBLIC GROUNDS LEST YOU SOW THE SEEDS OF T.B."(48) One who reads the story chuckles with laughter on seeing the distortion of the real and intended meaning of these signboards.

"The Quack" provides with another instance where Bhattacharya exhibits his sense of humour. The way-side quack, failing to sell his black powder to the people in the crowd, changes his tactics and announces that his powder is not a panacea for all diseases, but can cure only four types of ailments. The reader is amused to note that diseases listed by him are of such divergent nature that they cannot be cured by one single drug. The man befools the crowd by his shrewd and eloquent advocacy of the drug:

> Two words of warning I will breathe before I give my humbler *Salaam* to you all and depart. Do not take this powder for a cure-all. There is no such thing, the vendor of cure-alls makes monkeys of you. This powder can do only four things: cure stings and bites; kill belly-ache; ease headache; last of all, rubbed on the gums it can make loose tottering teeth return in the sockets and stand pillar-like.(102-3)

His description of the powder is humorous and arouses laughter.

VI

As regards the style and language of his fiction, Bhattacharya frequently makes experiments. Being an Indian writer, he has to convey through English the vast range of expressions, experiences and observations of the people whose awareness has been conditioned by languages other than English. While doing so, he is confronted, like other Indian English writers,[15] with the problem of handling the English language skilfully. He has, therefore, to take certain liberties with the normal diction and syntax of English in the process of his creativity.

While experimenting in diction, Bhattacharya very often renders the native proverbs and idioms literally in English. Through this device the novelist aims to achieve a linguistic success, giving a local colouring to the narrative without reducing its intelligibility. Moreover, these proverbs and idioms mark both the individuality and the Indianness of the characters who use them. Almost all his novels illustrate Bhattacharya's liberal use of the Indian proverbs and idioms. A few instances may be cited as under:

So Many Hungers

A rat slips in through a doorway too narrow for the bulky elephant. (62)

The crows will curse! (85)

Music for Mohini

They're like the tomcat who became an ascetic when he was too old and crippled to run after rats. (41)

You may be digging a canal from the river to your house door and inviting the crocodile. (39, 64)

Horses and camels find the stream bottomless, but the rat squaks. (55)

To a lotus pool the wary jeweller goes, and values the white blooms with his teststone. (87)

Pouring milk into a cracked pitcher. (18)

Words won't tie the air into the knots. (19)

He Who Rides a Tiger

A sparrow preens as a parrot. (15)

An ant grows wings and flies in the air. Does that make it a bird or even a moth? (92)

A Goddess Named Gold

A thousand mustaches can live together in amity but not four breasts! (42)

When there is smoke, there must be fire, when there is blood, there must be a body. (55)

A duck must swim and a rat steal grain. (108)

The two who sit on the same bough of a tree cannot hack off the bough. (162)

When an ass laments the loss of a cow, his guts will not pine for five drops of milk. (191)

He who eats honey out of a hive does not fear being stung. (290)

Shadow from Ladakh

One must wear painted plumes in the company of peacocks. (112)

Apart from proverbs and idioms, Bhattacharya often reproduces in English Bengali words and phrases as they are. The reader frequently finds in *So Many Hungers* words like "han," "nah," "are," "hoon," "magister," "policewala," "congresswala," "kisan," "Bhai," "Dakghar," "chal" (for *rice*), "dal" (for *pulses*), "sari," "Bhagwan," "prodeep" (for *lamp*), "Dhoti," etc. In *Music for Mohini*, one comes across words like "Didi," "Bhurja tree," "asirwad," "Swayamvara," "ashram," "Shehnai," "Ekadashi". *He Who Rides a Tiger* has "Baba," "Durga," "Khoka," "Lichees," "Jai Hind," "Pujari" (for priest), "Karma" (for destiny). *A Goddess Named Gold* uses "taveez," "Pan" (for betel), "Sona" (for gold), "Halwaii." In *Steel Hawk and Other Stories*, one finds words like "Kanchuli" (for brassiere), "Mahashilpi," "dharma," "Mantra," "Asadh" (a month), "Dagdar Sa'b," "Bitchchu"(for a scropion), etc.

Many hybrid compounds, joining English and native words, common in Indian conversation, have also been freely used by Bhattacharya in his writings. For instance, "Lamp-man," "Queen-mother," "Red turban," "cookwoman," "picture-play," "water-machine," "fire-engine," "Fire-wagon," "Flower-woman," "flower-bed," "head-protector," "joy-moments," "Old Mother" (for grandmother), "Rag-woman," "milk-sweet," "milk-infant," "tongue-clever," "sweet-shop" (for a vendor of sweets), "Cowhouse," "the spouse-of-all" (for a prostitute), "household king" (for a husband), "tooth-doctor" (for a dentist), etc.

Bhattacharya also ocassionally adds suffix "-ling" to certain words just to suggest their smallness or insignificance. Such words occur mostly in *So Many Hungers* and *A Goddess Named Gold*. Some of the examples are: "Childling," and "godling" (*So Many Hungers*), "frogling," "ghostling," "wifeling," "pigling," "starveling" and "goatling" (*A Goddess Named Gold*). Another device that the novelist commonly uses is of adding suffix " – ful" to certain adjectives. *So Many Hungers* has "belly-ful." *Music for Mohini* has "cheekful," "fistful" and "prideful" instead of the usual "proud."

Bhattacharya also makes literal translation of the Bengali pharses into English. Examples of such translated phrases can be found at random in the novels, especially, *So Many Hungers*, *Music for Mohini* and *A Goddess Named Gold. So Many Hungers* records phrases like "white as lime-plaster," (47) "greed in the belly," (52) "full upto the throat," (84) "in a muse," (48) "two moons were gone," (93) and "Just a way of talk," (97) etc. *Music for Mohini* has numerous examples: "get this plain feet in your stomach," (15) "eat by head," (17) "a cheekful of smile," (39) "The tree of marriage . . . was still barren" (162) and "Anger burned in her," (163) etc. In *A Goddess Named Gold*, he uses phrases like "a bellyful of good laugh," (24) "one of our own skin and sweat," (25) "flute-shaming voice" (12) and "you have made us noseless," (25) etc. This novel also illustrates some choice abusive epithets which are of the very stuff of colloquial speech, such as "brother of a bug," "brother of a cockroach" and "son of a city peacock," etc.

One more peculiar feature of Bhattacharya's language, a characteristic shared by other Indian languages, is that of "reduplicating a word with a change of initial sound."[16] The novelist may employ this device in various contexts, but the initial purpose is always to infuse colloquialism into the dialogue. "Khitir-mitir," (*So Many Hungers*) "vote-mote" and "Board-moard" (*A Goddess Named Gold*) and "Sona-Mona" (*Steel Hawk and Other Stories*) etc. serve the same end.

As mentioned earlier, Bhattacharya's experimentation in diction is aimed to create a peculiar effect: to impress on the reader the Indianness of the character, situation and expression in his novels. Though at times his English may appear quaint to the readers, yet he is normally successful in conveying the particular and specific reality through his novels with the help of an adopted language. In this regard, Bhattacharya is unlike Mulk Raj Anand who not only profusely uses the literally-translated Punjabi proverbs, swear-words and abuses in his fiction, but also unhesitatingly distorts the genuine English spellings of certain words (for instance, "yus" for yes, "notus" for *notice*, "injun" for *engine*, "gentreman" for *gentleman*, "phront" for *front* and "Laften gorner" for *Lieutenant Governor*). Anand's language appears somewhat unnatural and jarring even to a non-Punjabi speaking Indian reader. Bhattacharya, on the contrary, uses only simple words that are common in other Indian languages also. If there are certain seemingly uncommon usages, the writer qualifies them immediately, enabling the reader to comprehend them without any difficulty. For example, when Bhattacharya uses "dadu" for the first time in *So Many Hungers*, (21) he also writes Grandfather immediately after. Similarly 'Bau-ma" is followed by its standard English substitute, Daughter-in-law. (99)

Besides diction, Bhattacharya also makes experiments in syntax, and attempts to change the usual structure and rhythm of English sentences. It has been alleged that his sentences sometimes sound "archaic, even biblical"[17] like those of Raja Rao. But while archaism becomes a characteristic feature of Raja Rao's prose, Bhattacharya uses it only rarely. Raja Rao employs various stylistic devices to create the archaic note. He often makes his meaning ambiguous and his reading exasperating by the use of this device. Bhattacharya's endeavours in this direction, being much restricted, are less jarring. He uses archaisms like "thine," "Goodly" or "god forsooth" (Perhaps, "good forsooth")[18] which merely add to quaintness of the sentences. Another device to create archaic note in his novels is Bhattacharya's use of "be" in a few sentences. But he constructs such sentences very sparingly. In *Music for Mohini*, we often come across queer sentences like, "Wilful they be oxen like children. Beat them not, and see how they start fun," (74) and "At your age why be ashamed to deck yourself prettily?" (145) *He Who Rides a Tiger*, too, contains few sentences with archaic "be": "It is better that milk be given to starvelings." (120) Fortunately, this tendency does not dominate Bhattacharya's style and he avoids this type of distortion of the syntax in his fiction.

Perhaps the most remarkable device that Bhattacharya employs while experminting with syntax is his putting a question-mark to a simple assertive sentence, and thus suggesting that either the statement contains an implied question or the assertion is ambiguous in nature. Some examples will illustrate the point clearly:

So hard you toil, Onu Bhai, so much you reap; your arms do not ache? (*So Many Hungers*, 89)

Perhaps she had seen a picture somewhere, and it stayed on in her fancy? (115)

You too make fun of me? You are just like the rest? She bit her lip fiercely. (*Music for Mohini*, 113)

You wish that I stay buried in the temple? Forever? (*He Who Rides a Tiger*, 220)

She had really wanted a bowl of water to drink? Or it was a ruse to be alone with Meera and touch her sympathy? (*A Goddess Named Gold*, 182)

Leh's limit of our territory? (*Shadow from Ladakh*, p. 27)

You have enjoyed my talk? (188)

You're not suggesting he may renounce the world? (*A Dream in Hawaii*, 94)

That's okay with you honey? (169)

Harish does not trust me? ("Glory at Twilight," 21)

It's the flying wonder, you hear? ("Steel Hawk," 135)

Bhattacharya repeats this trait so often in his fiction that it becomes a very obvious attribute of his style. Actually, he tries to give a regional flavour to his language through this device, and he succeeds fairly well in his attempt. Meenakshi Mukherjee elucidates that this "peculiarity of style can be explained only in one way. In the Bengali language the form of a statement and that of a question are sometimes identical, the difference being indicated in speech through tone, and through punctuation in writing. Perhaps Bhattacharya deliberately tries to recreate the Bengali rhythm in the English language by doing away with the syntactic distinction between a question and a statement."[19]

One more notable feature peculiar to the Bengali language that Bhattacharya occasionally introduces in his English usage is the avoiding of the verb "to be" in some of the sentences. Had it been used sparingly, it would not have appeared very significant, but Bhattacharya repeats it so frequently that it becomes a significant characteristic of his style, and sometimes appears odd or unusual to a reader who is accustomed to the standard English idiom. Some striking instances may easily be cited here:

Trinklet! What use to me. You gone, who would look at them? (*So Many Hungers*, 106)

Mohini of age. Mohini, born on the night of Festive Lights and herself a light. (*Music for Mohini*, 19)

The glory! A worthy mistress of Behula. None like her in the hundred villages around. (150)

A pully-borne bucket under my feet. Five pairs of hands to pull me up. (*A Goddess Named Gold*, 67)

Two neighbours. India and China. Two neighbours again, Gandhigram and Steeltown. And the city planning to annex the village, not acres of earth alone but a way of life, an inner spirit. (*Shadow from Ladakh*, 73)

Bhattacharya also frequently uses a number of short sentences together. Through this device, he tries to introduce in his narrative the flavour of conversation in real life. The reader on such occasions appears to be listening to the characters talking or brooding. For example:

"You don't see her? Madame Bare-back! The woman with her back completely bare. A Hindu woman – so shameless!" . . .
Oh, that one? I know her. A curious story. Her husband is a colleague of mine. Not my own department. Chemistry. (*So Many Hungers*, 47)

A spirited girl! But I have charge of you. The tenderness in the face.. . . The battle in the eyes. We march together you and I. The easy comradeship. A new life to make. (*He Who Rides a Tiger*, 189)

A quarter-hour was gone. The impact was gone. Serenity filled him. His thoughts were lucid. (*A Dream in Hawaii*, 48)

There's another person you will meet. My Great-Uncle. He has gone for a walk. He is a bit crazy. Do not mind him. Just keep out of his way. ("My Brave Great-Uncle," 33)

Ordinarily the idea or the meaning that a number of short sentences brought together reflect, could have been conveyed only by long complex sentences. The novelist, however, follows this method even at the cost of the normal sentence structure, simply because it lends verisimilitude to his dialogues.

Although Bhattacharya freely experiments in diction and syntax of the English language, often violating the accepted norms, and altering the basic sentence patterns in his fiction, it should by no means be assumed that he does not write pure and standard English. He writes in his typical style and language only with a view to representing a different ethos. All the colloquialism and the literal redering of proverbs, phrases, idioms or words occurs for the most part in the dialogues between characters, and not in the novelist's own comments. Whenever he makes a direct statement, his language and style are poetic and impressive as will be evident from following examples:

> From the green carpet of the maidan, edged by the flower embroidery of the Curzon park, rose the fat thumb of Octerloney Monument to proclaim under a cloud-heavy sky the lithic strength of the Empire. Far to the south, near the river bank the mass of Fort William was a couchant lion. (*He Who Rides a Tiger,* 51)

> In the sweltering heat they sat on a shadeless bench and in silence they watched the river yellowed by the monsoon flood. A ferry boat chugged along to the opposite bank where factory chimneys were belching thick black smoke. Barges loaded with merchandise tossed about in the fast current. Close by, a flight of stone steps descending to the water was jammed with the people eager for a dip. (*A Dream in Hawaii*, 84)

Even when Bhattacharya makes his characters brood in privacy their thoughts are conveyed in an ornate style and compact language. For example:

> The frail plant with its brown, sweet-scented leaves was a mere emblem, she knew, vested with a mystic value, as a picture was or a pebble, moving the mind towards self suggestion, so that the inner eye should strip the veil of appearances and look beyond. (*Music for Mohini*, 102)

In fact, Bhattacharya's art and medium of expression remain growing slowly yet steadily to maturity from the very beginning of his creative career. This evolution becomes markedly evident in *Shadow from*

Ladakh. This novel, though studded with the extracts from Gandhi's writings, has been written in an eloquent prose style, and the language, too, is almost free from the dominating colloquialism of the preceding novels. The same stylistic eloquence runs through *The Steel Hawk and Other Stories*. Except for one or two instances where the writer attempts to innovate in matters of language by using sentences like "there was not an eye flick of time to lose" ("Steel Hawk," 135), there is no violation of the accepted English diction and syntax. In his latest novel, *A Dream in Hawaii*, Bhattacharya handles dexteroulsy both his theme and language. Like B. Rajan, he loads the sentences with meritriciousness. The idiom used in such cases is the standard English idiom, and the phrases and images are suggestive. Specific instances may be cited here:

> A firefly cannot be a star! (92, 234)
> the words pouring like water in a sunlit cataract. (8)
> a stone's throw from India. (110)
> Cracks in the mammoth structure. (19)
> Squeeze out the juice. (26)
> a colour in the rainbow. (144)
> A molehill looked like a mountain. (198)

At one or two places, the novelist also attempts to give an impression of archaism by citing from *The Bible*. For example "Blessed are the have nots, for they shall inherit the earth." (134) The language in this novel has been used articulately and figuratively. However, one peculiarity of the style in *A Dream in Hawaii* is that certain passages open aburptly, without having any regard or consideration for the normal syntax. The only possible and plausible explanation for this peculiarity may be that such passages reflect the internal monologues – unconscious thoughts of the characters. All said, this novel successfully established Bhattacharya as a perfect creative artist, endowed with a clear vision and masterly technical skill.

This detailed treatment of Bhattacharya's smithy reveals him as a master artist, constructing his plots artistically, creating his people realistically, narrating his stories interestingly and handling his prose dexterously. The use of symbolism and irony, an unfailing sense of humour and sincerity of purpose further enhance the appeal of his fiction which though dealing with the contemporary Indian life, has a wider and universal significance.

NOTES

1. Shiv K. Kumar and Keith Mckean, *Critical Approaches to Fiction* (New York: McGraw-Hill, 1968), p. 45
2. Forster, p. 116.
3. *Ibid.*, p.118.
4. Edwin Muir, *The Structure of the Novel* (New Delhi: B.I., 1979), p. 58.
5. Forster, p. 64.
6. R.S. Singh, *Indian Novel in English*, p. 107.
7. Sudhakar Joshi, p. vii.
8. *Ibid.*
9. *World Literature Written in English*, April 1972, pp. 95-108.
10. Lila Ray, p. 74
11. Chandrasekharan, p. 147.
12. Raji Narasimhan contends that Bhattacharya "sees Suruchi as a far more attractive figure physically. But the long-suffering, essentially patient conduct of Kasturba in the face of the excess of Gandhi is the same as Suruchi's. It only proves the existence in real life of the rudiments of the prototype that has been perfected in the mythical imagination. It serves to make Suruchi uncontrived in spite of the heavy romanticising and stilted treatment." *Sensibility under Stress: Aspects of Indo-English Fiction* (New Delhi: Ashajanak, 1976), p. 108.
13. Chandrasekharan, p. 146.
14. *Ibid.*, p. 147.
15. Raja Rao, too, recognizes the problem and admits in his "Foreword" to *Kanthapura*: "The telling has not been easy. One has to convey in a language that is not one's own the spirit that is one's own. One has to convey the various shades and omissions of a certain thought-movement that looks maltreated in an alien langauge. After language the next problem is that of style. The tempo of Indian life must be infused into our English expression, even as the tempo of American or Irish life has gone into the making of theirs."
16. Chandrasekharan, p. 153.
17. Meenakshi Mukherjee, *Twice-Born Fiction* (New Delhi: Arnold-Heinemann, 1974), p. 177.
18. *Ibid.*, p. 179.
19. *Loc.cit*

Bibliography

(a) Novels and Short-Stories

So Many Hungers. Bombay: Jaico, 1964.

Music for Mohini. New Delhi: Orient Paperbacks, 1952.

He Who Rides a Tiger. Delhi: Hind Pocket Books, 1954.

A Goddess Named Gold (1960). Delhi: Hind Pocket Books, 1968.

Shadow from Ladakh (1966). Delhi: Hind Pocket Books, 1968.

Steel Hawk and Other Stories. Delhi: Hind Pocket Books, 1968.

A Dream in Hawaii. Madras: The Macmillan (India), 1978.

(b) Other Writings

The Golden Boat (1932). Bombay: Jaico, 1970.

Indian Cavalcade. Bombay: Nalanda, 1948.

Towards Universal Man. London: Asia, 1962.

Gandhi the Writer: the Image as it Grew. New Delhi: NBT, 1969.

Mahatma Gandhi. New Delhi: Arnold-Heinemann, 1977.

Socio-Political Currents in Bengal: A 19th Century Perspective. New Delhi: Vikas, 1980.

(c) Articles in Books and Journals

"How I wrote *So Many Hungers*!" *Letteraturnaya Gazetta* (Moscow), 1951.

"Literature and Social Reality." *The Aryan Path* (Bombay), XXVI, ix, September 1955.

"The People of the Villages Change Their Theme." *The Times* (London), Jan. 23, 1961.

"Indo-Anglian." *The Novel in Modern India*, ed. Iqbal Bakhtiyar, Bombay, 1964.

"Baseless Prejudice against Indians Writing English." *The Statesman* (New Delhi), August 1968.

"A Bridge Between the People." *India and Southeast Asia: Proceedings of a Seminar.* New Delhi: Indian Council for Cultural Relations, 1968.

"Hollow Arbiters of the Writer's Destiny." *The Statesman* (New Delhi), May 1968.

"The Nature of Wisdom." *Abbottempo*. North Chicago: Abbot Universal, 1970.

"Woman in My Stories." *Journal of South Asian Literature* (Michigan), XII, iii-iv, Spring-Summer 1977.

Index